WHITE PEOPLE REALLY LOVE SALAD:

What My Childhood Taught Me About Diversity, Equity & Inclusion

WHITE PEOPLE REALLY LOVE SALAD:
What My Childhood Taught Me About Diversity, Equity & Inclusion
By: Nita Mosby Tyler, Ph.D.

Published by Nita Mosby Tyler, Ph.D.
www.theequityprojectllc.com

ISBN: 978-1-387-89102-3

DEDICATION

This book is dedicated to my parents,
John Mosby, Jr. and Barbara Hancock Mosby

You made me who I am today.
You have given me the tools to carry out equity, inclusion and
diversity work by using powerful stories that you helped to create in
my life. Your forward-thinking parenting is the reason I am able to
recall my childhood in such a meaningful way.

You were my first up-close-and-personal models for social justice.
You made sure I knew every step of my journey would be a
critical part of who I would later become.

You taught me that oppression was about the psyche of others;
I didn't have to claim it in my own psyche. I finally get it!
I love you. I love you. I love you.

I am forever grateful that I was blessed enough to be your daughter.
You have given me eternal content to learn from, grow from,
talk about and write about.

ACKNOWLEDGEMENTS

This book could not have happened without the support
and hard work of a great team. I'd like to thank the people
who helped to make *White People Really Love Salad*, a reality:

Rev. Dr. Timothy E. Tyler, my husband, soul-mate and best friend
who constantly encouraged me to document my stories to share
with the world. Thank you for being the chief catalyst in my life;
supporting me as I make my dreams come true. I love you...

Jasmine Elizabeth, my Vision Manager at The Equity Project, LLC,
who created timelines, strategy and brought the vision of this
book into reality. Thank you for pushing me to the
finish line with love and grace.

To The Equity Project, LLC and The HR Shop, LLC teams
for your undying support of my work. Thank you for
advancing this work in all that you do.

To Kumu Kandaswamy and Alex Koentges for being with
me from the very beginning as I launched The Equity Project, LLC.
and began to envision this book. You were with me when all of this
was just a dream. I couldn't have done any of this without you.

To Imani Baruti, Brea Zeise, Natalie Landau and Alex Goiran
for bringing the 1970's alive as the models for my book cover.
You helped me to set the stage for the title of the book
in the most realistic (and hilarious) way.

Thank you!

CONTENTS

INTRODUCTION

I think I have always had this book inside my head. My childhood stories have always been a large part of my life and as I have gotten older, the stories have become more vivid and much more poignant as I approach my work each day. As I look back on my life, it is clear that much about my theories, thoughts and musings about equity , inclusion and diversity were shaped during my childhood. There are direct correlations between childhood experiences and the lenses that I use to do equity work and even the biases that I have about people and systems.

I am amazed at the way in which my work has been shaped by random, episodic scenarios in my life. I had no idea that the often innocuous activities in my life would be shaped into direct and powerful ways to teach, strategize, advance and fight for systems of equity in our world. I could have never dreamed that what I did in kindergarten has helped me to mobilize equity work in one of the world's largest healthcare organizations or that grief would lead me to a life-changing conversation with a legendary civil rights leader. I was being a kid doing kid things. What I didn't know was that those "kid things" were the best education I could have ever gotten to be who I am today.

One of the toughest parts of advancing equity, inclusion and diversity in the world is that the work can be personally destabilizing if you, yourself, are not anchored in something that grounds you. For example, just like nursing, social work and law enforcement, equity work can create a secondary trauma; the kind of trauma where you begin to absorb the pain of those you are working with and for.

Because of our difficult racial history in the United States, oftentimes the mere mention of race creates a visceral reaction in those around us. This fatigue and trauma begins to kick in. When it does, we begin to question whether the work is too large…or if it is really our job to be involved in it…or even if it is worth it to get involved. In some cases we shut down; becoming disengaged from the work. To be anchored allows us to better focus on what part and quantity of the work we will be involved in and then proceed in doing that. The key is you have to balance yourself much like a footstool. You can't put your whole self in the work. That is a recipe for collapse. You should plant a part of yourself in what you are fighting for and the other part of yourself must always be anchored in other things you care about (community, family, church, etc.). When you are anchored beyond your work, you will find that you are more balanced (literally) and able to be the catalyst for much more. You will also find if things become difficult in what you are fighting for (one leg of the stool), because you are anchored elsewhere (the other two legs of the stool), it is easier to have peace and resiliency. Remember the three-legged stool as you think about your anchor. What does each leg represent in your life?

As I travel the country as a consultant and trainer, I work with organizations and communities who are working hard to advance equity, inclusion and diversity. The work is multi-faceted and requires finesse in understanding what we are actually attempting to course-correct. I find that our current socio-political climate has strained relationships, so we often point fingers at each other and miss, oftentimes, the need to focus on systems were racism is institutionalized and structural.

The reality is, to have an equity lens requires us to look at our systems, our people and our processes. More importantly, to have an equity lens requires us to go deep into our own experiences in understanding the source of our biases, stereotypes and thinking. I believe the cursory fashion in which we talk about bias has let us all off the hook in doing this deeper exploration. Saying "we all have biases" isn't helpful. It is true, but the exploration can't stop there.

I have found in my own exploration that these biases (and many other things) were shaped, to some degree, in my childhood. In this book, I explore thirty short childhood stories that represent how I came to be a leader in this field of work. Each story is a lesson and a testimony to the resiliency and aptitude of children as they take on very grown-up topics like race, oppression and even, death. I will share stories from age five to age twenty-two; each story given you a window into my development.

Enjoy the journey into my life. Some stories are funny. Others are hard to fathom. Do take the time to explore with me: jot down your own musings about what you've read. What did you see and feel in each story? What is your story? Equity calls for systems where everyone can thrive. Our collective stories are an important condition of that happening.

"

In advancing equity,
the goal is excellence;
not perfection.

"

Deconstructing Equity

Conversations about equity seem to be all the rave, but I have spent my life being a bit cynical about how we are having these conversations and frankly, how we are even defining the word. My life's work, as far back as I can remember, has been a constant quest for deeper more sustainable ways to institutionalize equity in a country that has institutionalized racism in its very fabric. Equity, to me, is creating systems where everyone can thrive. Not for some people. For all people.

The iterative and sometimes, prescribed, way in which we moved in this country from discussions related to diversity to discussions related to inclusion to then, discussions related to equality and then to equity (and let's not forget conversations about fairness and justice) has unequivocally and thoroughly confused everyone. Now, when the average person hears the word "equity" it is easy to imagine the definition of "equality." The same holds true for the word "diversity." When we hear it, we sometimes see it as about the same thing as "inclusion" - *whatever that means.*

Most certainly, when we hear the word "diversity" our minds go straight to race. I call diversity, inclusion, equality and equity **The Power Four**. They are the four words that have the capacity to either make us or break us. They (with our help, of course) can create great structures or institutionalize hate. It's up to us.

It is important for us to focus on deconstructing these component parts of equity to help us understand what we're actually seeking to change. The term-confusion we experience has made operationalizing change incredibly difficult. This book is designed to help us to understand what each of the elements of equity means in theory and in practice.

I will do this through stories; some told from the voice of a kindergartener.

As I was writing this book, I recalled the many points in my life that perfectly described the pure definitions of either diversity, inclusion, equality or equity. I thought of the ways in which *The Power Four* had shown up. In some cases, it really was as early as kindergarten. Although we tend to talk about *The Power Four* most often when we describe our workplaces and communities, it is critical that we think more simply about these structural parts of how we build and behave within systems. The reality is all of these elements show up as early as childhood and will shape how we build or collapse systems of equity later in life. There isn't a day that goes by that I don't liken today's experiences, in particular, around race, power, equity and gender to something that I learned as a child. I am equipped to deal with today's issues because I probably dealt with them in kindergarten.

Some of the complexity of understanding *The Power Four* rests squarely with how we screwed up the definition of diversity when we begin to socialize the term heavily in the 1980's. If you think about it, the 1980's was filled with opportunities to help others wrap their head around diversity. During the 1980's, we had the HIV/AIDS epidemic, the War on Drugs/crack cocaine epidemic, more women moving into leadership roles, more people of color coming into the workforce, Reaganomics, more vocal discussion about Affirmative Action, continuation of the normalizing of integration…the list goes on and on. The best that most organizations could do at the time (and I know this because I was a diversity trainer during this time) was create cursory phrases for all to embrace, like:

- Value Diversity
- Embrace Diversity
- Tolerance (which, by the way, is what we do when babies cry on airplanes. Not really what I recommend we say to describe diversity)

We even had bumper stickers that said these things. We simply wanted people to get on board with the changing demographics of communities and workplaces; and quick! The problem was the way we went about engaging them was a bit of a travesty. In my opinion, there were two great travesties that occurred in the 1980's that set us on a path of confusion that we are still tackling today. In many ways, these travesties are what helped to create the barriers we have today in advancing systems of equity.

The Travesty of What We Did to White People in Diversity Training in the 1980's

During the onset of mass diversity training (you know… the mandatory kind that made the hair on the back of your neck stand up when you found out you had to go), the workplaces and subsequently, the classes in the 1980's were largely white audiences. The classes were designed at the time to explain and normalize the term diversity and to encourage all of us to have open minds and hearts about differences.

The travesty of this story was the way in which we described and defined the word diversity during training. For the most part, we described diversity, explicitly, as ***everything that wasn't white***. Of course, we know this is an incorrect definition of diversity, but at the time, we over-highlighted diversity as being all things not white. Because of this, we created a scenario in which white people were not included in opportunities to discuss their stories, ancestry or lineage. It was if they were void of history. Our focus during the 1980's was still largely on race, so in the context of this travesty, we also ill-defined the word diversity as something that served as a synonym for race. This is why today, when most people hear the word diversity, their minds immediately go to race. Diverse communities. Diverse candidates. These terms all take us to race; something other than white. It is "othering" at its best.

The Travesty of What We Did to People of Color in Diversity Training in the 1980's

The travesties didn't stop with white audiences; there were travesties that impacted people of color present in those same educational settings. As we defined the word diversity, it was clear that it was a description of people of color – we were explicit about that. The travesty was that in defining the word diversity, we only described the oppressions of people of color. We didn't discuss the contributions, inventions or values of people of color. This oppression-based way to describe diversity polarized groups; setting up the realities of a perpetrator-victim model. Again, it created a scenario where diversity became the code word for race in a country that still had institutional and structural issues with racism. An issue we are still struggling with today.

Where Do We Start to Truly Understand Equity?

As simple as it sounds (it isn't…), many of our answers come from what happened to us as children. Our cues and signals about race or identity may have been developed from the games we played, the activities we were involved in or the messages we heard as children. Whatever the case, where we came from is worth revisiting as we explore where we need to go. In this book, I will take you on a journey of some important milestones in my childhood. These milestone moments have shaped who I am today – both good and bad. This book will illustrate the poignant nature of our simplest childhood experiences; shaping the very complicated beliefs, consciousness and actions that are a part of who we are as adults today. Equity can be intrinsically connected to child's-play.

Each short story in this book describes a very prominent scenario in my childhood. The stories are prominent in my life because I have complete clarity about how each scenario has shaped the adult that I am today. As you read the book, I encourage you to begin thinking of stories of your own childhood – good times and bad times. These stories will become the lens by which you will ultimately advance diversity, equity, equality and inclusion in the world.

After each story, I will share my musings about the story. It is here that I will connect the dots or translate what the story actually represents from an equity lens. I will then invite you to create your own musings about the story. What does the story represent to you? How can/does the story connect to the way in which you might see relationships, challenges or barriers in the world? Capturing your musings gives you an opportunity to reflect and explore more deeply about what you're reading.

My Musings:

Equity starts with understanding the definitions of diversity, inclusion, equality and equity. They don't mean the same things. In order to advance and achieve equity we must understand how inequity shows up in our systems. As much as it feels easier to point out <u>people</u> who represent "the problem," we must get to the point where we can just as easily point out <u>systems</u> that perpetuate or even cause "the problem." We have to understand that there is no U.S. system that was built with equity in mind. Education, healthcare, the justice system, housing, the list goes on and on. None of them were built with all of us in mind. This is critical because these are precisely the systems we will need to collapse, augment, amend or chip away at to get to *systems where everyone can thrive*. That, by the way, is my definition of equity.

Your Musings:

_____

_____

_____

_____

In the Beginning

Growing up in the segregated South was not easy, but my parents had a knack for sheltering me from the hardness of the times. The 1960's and 1970's in Atlanta, Georgia were a time of both pain and evolution and I grew up seeing the best and the worst of it all. I recall seeing the last vestiges of the Colored and Whites-only water fountains; expressing often and loudly to my mother that it was ridiculous. She nodded meekly as I watched her normalize one of the most hateful artifacts of modern history. My father, a transplant from Middletown, Ohio, a sleepy Mayberry-like town between Dayton and Cincinnati, didn't understand how the South and the North could be so different. He experienced integrated neighborhoods and decent racial relationships growing up in Middletown and was now watching "reasonable, religious, educated Georgians" fight, cross-burnings and all, to keep Black people out of neighborhoods and schools. Unlike my mother who lived in Atlanta her entire life and who came to accept social lunacy as "the way things were," my father had no problem denouncing what he saw. It was through my father's eyes and voice that I begin to understand differences, hope and activism. The world was telling me and showing me that I was not included, I was less than and I didn't belong. My father was telling me to soar, to keep my head up, to be the boss. His message made more sense to me than that of the world. I chose him.

Growing up Black in the South was filled with complexity from the inside out. Much of it was told in stories from my mother. She was the first person in her family to earn a college degree. Quite an accomplishment for the times. She attended Clark Atlanta University, an HBCU (historically Black College & University) in Atlanta. Fondly, she attended college with friends she had been in school with since first grade. Just recently when my mother turned 80 years old, many of those friends attended her birthday party. The longevity of friendships mired in social lunacy and oppression amaze me. I feel the power of my rich ancestry each time I am among my mother and her friends.

My mother didn't have an easy childhood. She was the oldest of four siblings and lived with my maternal grandparents in a two-bedroom rented duplex on what would later become Martin Luther King, Jr. Drive in Atlanta, Georgia (…it began as Hunter Street). My maternal grandmother was adamant that she and my grandfather would do whatever it took to send my mother to college. My maternal grandmother, a seamstress at the Ruston Company, a major producer of stuffed animals and toys and my maternal grandfather, a painter and maintenance technician at Georgia Tech University worked hard to make ends meet even without a college education, but they did it. My mother went to college and graduated in the height of the ugliness of the Civil Rights Movement. She moved her tassel from the right to the left and became what I came to know as a first-generation oppressed scholar.

My father didn't have an easy childhood either. He was the youngest of two siblings and lived in a stately house in Middletown, Ohio. My paternal grandmother was a domestic worker; a maid for a wealthy banking family in Middletown. I never met my paternal grandfather. He died before I was born. My paternal grandmother married again, but I never met him either. My grandmother worked hard as a single-mother, sometimes even rotating her days working as a maid with her sisters so she could have time with her sons. My father completed 10th grade and went into the Air Force, never graduating from high school. He proudly served as a member of the military police. My father's oldest brother went off to attend Morehouse College in Atlanta, Georgia. This prominent Historically Black College & University (HBCU) was particularly top-notch (we called it the Black Ivy-League of the times), so the family celebrated his admission. My father, who looked up to his older brother, was equally proud. But, not as proud as my grandmother. She even told

12

people in town that my father's brother had gone off to Morehouse to be a doctor. I always wondered why people in town called him "Doc." No one ever told them he wasn't – including my grandmother.

My parents met on the Atlanta University campus; my father made a trip from Middletown to Atlanta to visit his brother at Morehouse College. My father had absolutely no business on the campus outside of waiting for his older brother to get out of class. It was one of those "let's hang out" moments that younger brothers desire and older brothers detest. My father roamed the campus, aimlessly, as he waited for his brother. As destiny would have it, he of all the people on that college campus, ran into my mother as she was coming from one of her classes. The rest is history. And history it was.

My father never went back to Ohio. Although the woman his mother wanted him to marry was there in Middletown; my father had different plans and Middletown didn't seem to be a part of it. The courtship of my parents was a beautiful one. My mother's friends and family adored him, and he adored them back.

My maternal grandparents loved him too. They were fascinated with this "northerner" and his tenacity and grace. He always had a strong desire to help others and it was evidenced in the way he treated my maternal grandparents. My mother recounts the story of what happened when my father first witnessed that my grandparents still had an icebox; not a refrigerator. He found an icebox to be prehistoric and wanted desperately for my grandmother to have a refrigerator. He went to an appliance store and began secretly making payments, on a layaway plan, towards the purchase of a new refrigerator for her. When he had paid it off, he had it delivered to my grandparent's home. When the delivery man showed up, my grandmother was confused and said there must be some mistake. The delivery man shared that the refrigerator was from my father – the man who loved my mother and clearly loved them, too.

My mother graduated from Clark Atlanta University and began her 40-year career as an elementary school teacher. My father took a job as an assemblyman at General Motors and eventually rose to the role of foreman. As they began their new careers, they also began their lives together as husband and wife. Their wedding, a small intimate affair with friends and family, was the beginning of a life filled with joy, pain, lessons and insights that shaped everything that happened from that day forward. About a year later, one of the things that came about was me. I was born November 12, 1962.

My parents were a well-oiled machine; my mother worked days and my father worked nights. My father determined that there was no daycare center in America that was good enough for me. His solution was to babysit me himself since he was home during the day. He had no reservations about this even though he would have worked all night. My father was determined and my mother complied. There you have it. My father was now the daycare center with zero hours sleep. This arrangement sounded good in theory. That is until the day my playpen caught fire because I scooted it over towards the floor furnace while he was sleeping. The playpen – the contraption designed to keep me safe and secure in case my father fell asleep, was now a smoking inferno because I was beginning to learn the power of scooting. My father awakened from his sleep because he smelled smoke. Luckily, he saved me from what would have been a devastating accident. As only my father could do, he remedied the entire situation, so it would never happen again. He suppressed my ability to scoot by tying my playpen to the couch with a belt. No more movement. He had reengineered a potential catastrophe in my life – the first of many he would be involved in.

This childcare arrangement continued until I was ready for kindergarten. My mother would come home exhausted from teaching 2nd graders all day and proceed to prepare dinner, take over childcare duty and pack my father's lunch as he got in a nap before it was time for his night shift at General Motors to begin. My mother had her hands full, as her presence meant my ability to scoot was once again restored. She allowed me to roam more freely and she enjoyed seeing the happiness that brought me. That is until the day she was on the

phone with one of her girlfriends as she was preparing dinner and she heard a blood-boiling scream from the living room. The living room. Where my dad was napping on the couch and the place I had scooted off too quickly without my mother noticing. I managed to find the floor furnace (again), but this time I was standing on it. It burned me so quickly that I couldn't lift my feet off it. My mother ran in from the kitchen and my father jumped up from the couch in a sleeping stupor, both grabbing me off the furnace. The burns were so severe that my skin was still on the grate of the furnace. The burns were so bad that I still have the permanent scars on the bottom of my feet today – 50+ years later. Grille marks. My original tattoo.

Among other things, these safety issues were the signal that it was time for our family to move into a more modern house – one void of floor furnaces. It was one of those 1960's moments where the pain of segregation and oppression was blended with the promise of progress evolving in Atlanta. Though times were still strained, we had an opportunity to move to suburbia – a neighboring community outside of Atlanta called Decatur. "White flight" was happening in full force in this community. White people were moving further out into Decatur and other suburban areas, leaving small, but established homes behind. My parents bought our new house from a white woman who thought it would be perfect for us because "lots of good coloreds like us were in the community." Our community was 100% Black and mostly blue-collar working families with children. I guess we were all good coloreds. Whatever that meant.

My Musings:

It is clear that these complex times in our U.S. history created what I call "cocooning" in our family. In a broader context of societal hate (relative to race relations during this time), my parents compensated by turning fully inward for the protection of our family. My parents created a cocoon; a safety zone within

our home. They decided they were most capable of protecting each other – at all costs. They did not let the outside in and they certainly didn't force themselves to have to be a part of the outside. They created workarounds to attempt to keep me safe. Safety became tethering me close to my father – even if he was asleep. Freedom became untethering me from that same scenario – an independence that I cherished. All of this was a protective, defense mechanism. What I learned from this story is that cocooning is not sustainable. It can leave room for unintended harm. It can serve as a way to minimize hurt, trauma and pain in the short-term but it doesn't eradicate it.

I was beginning to, subconsciously, learn that the world was unfair and what was outside of my house was out to get me. I was learning that no matter what, safety might not be possible. I was also learning that maybe freedom was impossible, too. I learned that there is pain in safety measures and pain in freedom measures. At some point, in either area – something hurts and something could certainly go wrong.

I also was beginning to learn that being "validated" by white people meant something in America. We were "good coloreds." That must be a good thing?

Your Musings:

_____

_____

_____

_____

_____

_____

_____

_____

Prelude with Prescott Penn

Kindergarten was fascinating, as it had a historic and complicated backdrop. The University Homes Nursery and Kindergarten had the historic Atlanta University as its backdrop, while at the same time ultimately sharing a name with one of Atlanta's largest housing projects. I loved school at an early age. Most of it came from sharing a house with an educator for a mother. The other came from my father, the 10th grade dropout, who valued my education more than anything in the world. There was no boundary between school and home. My mother never stopped teaching. We even had a bulletin board in our house and we had to recite poetry at the dinner table. The teaching never ended.

My kindergarten classroom was predominately Black. It drew kids from the surrounding community neighborhoods and it included some kids like me, the early Black suburbanites who still identified and were aligned with life in the city. Even though we had moved to a suburb of Atlanta, our social structures like church, hair salons, friends, etc. were still in the city. Our families knew each other. They played, prayed and even worked together. School was family. School was community – no matter where we lived.

Kindergarten was an important milestone in my life because it was the first time I developed a relationship with someone of a different race. I'm sure I knew people came in different colors (my parents did a good job, early on, of teaching me about differences), but I am certain I did not have friendships, feelings or even love for people who were other colors. That is until I met Prescott Penn. Prescott was an Asian boy in my kindergarten class. He stuck out quite a bit in the sea of Black 4 and 5-year old faces in the class, but he didn't seem to mind. Neither did we. He was funny-looking to us because he was different. He was one of us and that is all we knew. The only diversity we knew about was being 5 years old. That's it.

Prescott and I formed a special bond. I seemed to sense when he didn't feel included. Oftentimes this was self-inflicted. He just pulled back and cried. I never knew why he was doing this and he couldn't quite tell me either. He would just say he didn't know why he was crying. I already thought boys were strange, but this one took the cake. Why would he not want to be a part of the group all of a sudden? I deduced that he was fairly pitiful even though he was one of us. On this particular day, during one of those moments when Prescott was feeling sad, he whispered in my ear that I was his girlfriend. Imagine that. On second thought…don't. I wasn't interested in being chosen.

The announcement of this new relationship status seemed to make Prescott a little happier. If he didn't feel attached to the whole group, he could now just feel attached to me. He got to share me with no one. He only wanted us to play together. It was like 5-year old privilege in a way.

One Monday morning when my mother dropped me off at school, as was commonly done, the teacher took time to commend students who had done a great job the previous week. I was one of those students. Actually, it seems I was always one of those students. I grinned with pleasure and humility as the class clapped. As we prepared for recess, Prescott whispered in my ear that "we" were going to run away from kindergarten. I looked at him in amazement, only to get a very serious look in return. He told me we should see where else we could go to school. A better place. Like the white people. It was a compelling thought, in a 5-year old kind of way. Why not?

During recess, Prescott and I snuck out of the playground through an opening in the fence. We left filled with wonder; me and Prescott. We roamed through broad territory (which was likely about a city block). We saw the woes of city life; homelessness, alcoholism and some things we weren't even old enough to categorize. We were free, untethered and excited on our quest to find the white experience. That is, until we heard the harsh screaming of our teacher and other staff calling our names. To get back to school. Right now. And we hadn't even found the white people yet!

My life changed that day. The student who received applause for doing such a great job last week was now standing in front of the entire class. Positioned for a paddling. Pants pulled down. Standing next to Prescott Penn. Humiliated while the class laughed. Oppressed and diminished and hating Prescott Penn on every level. I remember after that having a bad feeling; a trauma of sorts, every time I saw an Asian kid. They would always remind me of how Prescott ruined my kindergarten life that day.

My Musings:

I was learning a bit about diversity – the richness and the beauty of the differences in all of us. Though my class was predominately Black, Prescott presented another area of learning for me. He wasn't quite white, but he certainly wasn't Black. His "in-between-ness" taught me about the differences in our differences. Prescott only went to our kindergarten because he had a parent who taught on the nearby college campus. For the most part, the rest of us went there because we weren't allowed to go to schools with white children. He wasn't white, but I was learning that there was a real hierarchy when it came to color. Interestingly, running away to go to a white school was nothing I had ever thought about. However, even at 5 years old, Prescott was already established in his thinking that a white school would be better. Not only had he formulated this thinking; encouraging me to do the same. He was also willing to challenge every known boundary to get there.

The other thing I was learning was bias. Getting in

trouble with Prescott caused me to lose my status of being a good student. Reminds me of being validated as a "good colored" by the white woman we bought our house from. Did this mean I was losing that status, too? This was a double-whammy. Now, someone else that didn't look like me was causing me pain and humiliation. The system of oppression in America was working and now Prescott was a part of it. I was losing.

For years after that day, when I saw anyone that looked like Prescott, it was a constant reminder of that terrible day in my kindergarten class. This was the prelude for both explicit and implicit bias. A sometimes-unconscious bias that likely prevented me from having meaningful relationships with other Asian people when I was younger.

Your Musings:

_____

_____

_____

_____

_____

_____

_____

_____

_____

_____

_____

_____

_____

_____

_____

_____

"

I am not sure we
included white people
in the definition of
diversity. And when
you don't include
people in the definition
of diversity, then
you can't jump to
inclusion, which is
exactly what we did.
"You're always going
to have an 'us vs. them'
if it's built that way.

"

Becoming Miss Ann

Georgia seemed to be slow on the draw with its acceptance of civil rights and integrated spaces. I still remember the number of places we would try to go to that still said they "didn't accept Negroes." My parents despised this. I could see it in their eyes. But, they would never talk about what it meant. I believe, in their own way, they didn't want me to establish the same feelings of hate for white people that they felt coming from white people. In their minds, the easiest way to ensure this was to never speak poorly about what was going on. I suppose they would rather I draw my own conclusions. I did.

As a 5-year-old, I was very interested in ballet. It seemed to be the 5-year-old-girl thing to do during those times. When we moved to suburban Decatur, my mother thought it was a good opportunity to enroll me in ballet school. You know, the kind where the teachers talked about all of your gifts and talents knowing that you'd never be a ballerina. We arrived at the first dance school and they told us, nicely, that they did not accept Negroes. We got back in the car as if we'd just gone to a grocery store that was out of orange juice. We said nothing and just got back in the car to head to the next ballet school. This school, in downtown Decatur, also said they didn't accept Negroes. At this point, I was confused. I asked my mother why they wouldn't take me and she said, "because they are not smart enough to accept you right now. They don't know how excellent you are." I had no idea what that meant, but I was sure it wasn't good. I could see it in my mother's eyes. She was angry, but it looked like she was on the verge of tears. I decided ballet was dumb. I had to think that to make sense of it all.

During a day at kindergarten, our teacher introduced us to

a beautiful, tall white woman named Miss Ann. I thought she was the prettiest white lady I'd ever seen. Even prettier than those I saw on TV. She was slender, with red lipstick, hair in the ballerina bun and she even had on her leotard, tights and tutu. I was mesmerized. Our teacher said Miss Ann was going to start teaching ballet classes right there at our school. Miss Ann introduced herself to us and said she was proud to be our dance teacher. It was unreal.

You see, what I know now is Miss Ann came to our school because she was fully aware that the white ballet schools would not accept Black girls. She was incensed by this and decided she would come to the Black neighborhood and teach the classes herself. It took courage, a justice consciousness and love for her to do this. All of a sudden, I didn't think ballet was dumb anymore. Miss Ann taught me a great deal about equity. Where there was no system of justice; she built one. We all thrived because of it. My hope was to become Miss Ann in all that I would do in my life. She is one of the most powerful symbols of why I do equity work today.

My Musings:

Miss Ann was my inspiration and muse in developing a social justice consciousness. She was an unlikely player – no one expected to see a white woman leading the way in this way. Miss Ann also taught me that <u>equity</u> **–** *creating systems where everyone can thrive and where everyone gets what they need* **– calls for courage, commitment and the aptitude and desire to create new doorways for others. More importantly, what Miss Ann did was create a system of** <u>equality</u>**. If the system didn't allow us to have the same as everybody else, she was determined to create an alternate system. I learned that** *equality is about access. Giving people a way in.* **My Blackness did not give me a way in, so Miss Ann just created a new door.**

Your Musings:

Winning or Losing?

Being the only child made it easy for me to be my parent's favorite project. I was involved in everything and was encouraged to be excellent in all that I did. I didn't mind this. The attention was fortifying. I was at the end of my kindergarten journey and looking forward to going to school with the big kids. I felt comfortable with the older kids, having frequently attended school with my mom; sitting in on her 2nd grade classes. I admired the maturity (don't laugh) of 2nd grade girls. They had pretty dresses and shoes and seemed to value that a lot more than kindergarten girls. I couldn't wait to get there.

One of the last events in my kindergarten journey was the May Day festival. It was a very big deal. There would be a May Day queen and king and all sorts of activities. I was so excited and was even more excited to find out that I would be a contestant in the May Day pageant. Even though I was the almost-graduated-kindergartener, I envisioned myself as the queen. Mature and regal like the 2nd graders in my mother's class.

Over the next few months, all I can remember is my mother feverishly working with my maternal grandmother to get my pageant dress. They would go back and forth between whether my grandmother would make it or if they would buy it. I didn't care. I just wanted to be a beautiful queen. I had never seen a Black queen before and I was going to be her. I begged my mother to let me wear my hair down; not in my typical pigtails. I reminded her that queens didn't wear pigtails. I reminded her that white girls wore their hair down. She was not moved by my reminders.

When I arrived at the May Day pageant, I felt beautiful. I had on a gorgeous yellow dress with a large crinoline underneath

to make the dress stand out. My grandmother bought it at Rich's Department Store in downtown Atlanta; her favorite store. I had on matching ruffled socks and patent leather shoes. My mother even managed to let me wear my not-so-long hair down. I truly felt like a queen. When I got to the pageant, my eyes were immediately drawn to my friend Vickie, another Black kindergartener, who was also in the pageant. Vickie and I were the best of friends. As happy as I was to see her, as I looked at her, all of a sudden, I felt like someone had pulled the rug out from under me.

All of a sudden, I felt ugly and plain. Vickie wore a floor length gown. Like the white girls on the Miss America pageant. Her dress was white, flowing and beautiful. She even had on a dab of red lipstick. Like the white girls on the Miss America pageant. Her hair, much longer than mine, was worn down with soft curls. Like the white girls on the Miss America pageant. She looked like an angel. Dolled up. Her skin a few shades lighter than mine. In my eyes, like the white girls on the Miss America pageant.

Vickie won the May Day pageant. I was 1st runner-up.

I lost. I cried for an eternity because no expensive dress from Rich's or ruffled socks could ever make my skinny legs, kinky hair and dark skin white. And in my mind to win meant being white even when you were Black. If they didn't like you, you couldn't get in. Everywhere I looked this was the case. Losing was becoming the norm. At five years old, I was beginning to understand my blackness in very complicated ways.

My Musings:
I was beginning to learn about something called colorism. My societal context was complicating my perception of worth based on race, but now I was learning that the shades/hues of color represented something too. I was learning that lighter skin was somehow better or prettier because it was closer to white. My darker skin felt like a liability. My mother had light skin and I thought she was beautiful. I determined that she was privileged because of this. My father had a very dark complexion. I remember thinking how cool it was that he was that popular with that very dark skin. I saw that as an anomaly. I was beginning

to formulate ideas about the model of beauty and attractiveness. This was the makings of discord for me both outside and inside of my very own race. White become the model for beauty as I was sinking in the complexities of my Black skin.

Your Musings:

_____

_____

_____

_____

_____

_____

_____

_____

_____

_____

_____

_____

_____

_____

_____

_____

_____

_____

_____

_____

_____

_____

"

If we don't tackle
institutional and
structural racism,
it will be impossible
to advance equity
work…it will be a
moot point. Ending
one is a condition of
developing the other.

"

Brown is the New Black

Entering 1st grade was a magical time. We were settling into our new suburban lifestyle and our community was strong and vibrant. It was great attending school with people that lived right on my street. It made this new experience a little less scary. I attended an elementary school with children that looked just like me. Our familiar faces made going to a new school easier to navigate. The albatross in the situation was the stark juxtaposition of race when observing my teachers. Not a single teacher was Black like me. Though we lived in a time where those "in charge" were typically white, I did wonder how these teachers could love me. That was, in my experience, what teachers were supposed to do. At least they did in kindergarten.

My 1st grade teacher was Mrs. Brown; a stern and rigid white woman who wore cat-eyed glasses and business suits. I had never seen a woman quite like her before. She was formal and had the most piercing eyes; even through her glasses. I quickly deduced that our class was an irritant to her. She didn't seem at all interested in us as individuals and was most often more concerned about getting the tasks at hand completed by whatever means necessary. I don't even know if she knew our names. Unlike kindergarten, the move to a more militarized academic experience was stunning. We were required to stand in line for everything, raise our hands for everything and sit and stand for everything. I remember when we received our vaccinations at school. We even stood in line for that while a school nurse went down the line shooting each one of us with what she called a "vaccination gun." It looked like a gun and it shot the injection right into our small arms. One by one – shot…shot… shot. It was traumatizing and the wailing and crying in anticipation of the shot was almost unbearable – no one to hold us and tell us it would be alright. There was no identifiable love for us. Sometimes, Mrs. Brown even refused to let us go to the restroom when we asked. I remember having my first "accident" because of this. I was sharply shamed, and I experienced a hurt that I never wanted to feel again.

It was maddening to have classroom experiences so impersonal that the activities seemed rote. I didn't even have to think about why I was doing what I was doing. It was just the expectation

to do it. We were robotic little Black children; simply following the latest command.

Mrs. Brown rarely referred to us by our names. She used a special term to reference us. She called us nincompoops. This was a word I had never heard before, but she used it constantly. It became so normalized that we even began to refer to each other by this name; even though we had no idea what it meant. She would call us nincompoops when we were being disruptive and she would call us nincompoops when she scolded us. Sometimes I think she simply called us nincompoops because she had not bothered to learn our names.

I learned quickly that I did not like this name. I didn't want to be a nincompoop – whatever it meant. I worked hard to please

Mrs. Brown; to get myself out of the category of nincompoop. I had no idea that this experience would set me on a life course of always trying to detach myself from any semblance of nincompoop-ness. I had no idea I was learning about the precursor for the "N-word" at 6 years old.

My Musings:

1st grade set the stage for the way in which I interpreted my value in the world. I learned quickly that I needed to do all that I could to please my white teacher because she didn't believe any of us were of value, special or smart. This was quite the contrast from how I was valued at home and in my community. I was loved and my community celebrated how special all of the kids were. People that looked like me seemed to love me. I believed, in many ways, I was invisible to my teacher. Mrs. Brown taught me to question my worth. This lesson, unfortunately, has stayed with me most of my life. Always questioning. Often wondering what the white person thinks about my mere existence. Always wondering if I am invisible to white people. Often contemplating my value in the world.

Your Musings:

_____

_____

_____

_____

_____

_____

_____

_____

Looking for White Brownies

My mother had a special knack for making sure I was as involved as possible in all kinds of activities. As a teacher, she had the inside track on all of the possibilities for extracurricular involvement, so she was always filled with what she called "great opportunities" for me. On this particular day, she came home and was very excited about introducing me to the world of Girl Scouts. Of course, I had heard of the Girl Scouts, mostly the cookies, but I had never thought about being one. I normally saw white Girl Scouts selling cookies outside the local grocery store. Nothing about that sounded like fun to me, but my mother said it would be great.

As only my mother could do, I found myself being driven to my first troop meeting. My mother shared that I would meet new friends and we would have a lot of fun together. When we pulled up at the troop meeting location, I remember having butterflies. I was a little nervous about joining a group of girls I didn't know. I walked in with my mother. The room was filled with little Black girls that looked just like me. They were all in uniforms – little brown uniforms and hats. They wore brown knee socks and patent-leather shoes. I had never seen anything like it. Everything was brown. They were brown. Their outfits were brown. Their socks were brown. What kind of Girl Scouts were these?

I looked at my mother in a bewildered way. She could always read my mind. She whispered to me that this was a troop of Brownies – a part of the Girl Scout family. I was horrified! Why on earth would they name this group of Black girls, Brownies? I wanted no part of this. Where were the white Brownies? *Were* there white Brownies?

Needless to say, my scouting career didn't last long. My mother was exhausted from the turmoil she had to go through as she dressed me for each troop meeting. I cried and cried when it was time for the meetings. I didn't want to wear the brown outfit and I didn't want to be called a Brownie. My behavior finally wore my mother down. She finally pulled me out of the troop. I sure was happy that I didn't have to be called Brownie anymore. And, I never found any white Brownies, either.

My Musings:

Color was beginning to take on a whole new meaning for me. Almost subconsciously, I was beginning to associate darkness to badness. Black and brown were taking on a negative connotation. Segregation was beginning to leave a lot to the imagination. Where I didn't have the complete story, I simply filled in the blanks. Race and racism was becoming a more complex puzzle that made me question the validity of everything. Was our Brownie motto and pledge legitimate if little white girls were contradicting everything that it said? I was learning to distrust major systems and organizations. One at a time, I was learning that everything wasn't exactly as it seemed.

Your Musings:

_____

_____

_____

_____

_____

_____

_____

_____

_____

_____

_____

"

We know that we have an equity problem in all of our major systems — education, health care, the justice system. Given who you are, your experience can be completely different than the person who comes right after you, and that's what we've got to reconcile.

"

"Is the Cereal Ready, Yet?"

Saturday mornings were always my favorite day of the week. I loved Saturday morning cartoons and I loved having both my parents there at home at the same time. Just like Christmas morning, I woke up on Saturday mornings just as the sun would rise. I couldn't wait to begin my ritual. Cereal and cartoons. The only real issue was I wasn't old enough to fix (or reach) the cereal, so I relied on my parents to be a part of this process. I was very fortunate that I had my own television set – a small black and white television that sat on my dresser. I was all set to watch the mornings first set of cartoons. I just needed my cereal to complete the process.

When my television was all set for the appropriate cartoons, I'd trek over to my parent's bedroom. My father slept on the side of the bed closest to the door, so I would get to him first. I would whisper in his ear, "Is the cereal ready?" This was my subtle way of encouraging him to get up and fix the cereal. At the crack of dawn, my father's response was always, "No. It isn't ready yet." He wouldn't even open his eyes or roll over. This would happen about four more times that same morning before my father would actually get up to fix the cereal. Each time he would answer, "No. It isn't ready yet." Each time he wouldn't open his eyes or roll over. But, when he finally got up to fix the cereal, it was magical.

He poured the cereal in the bowl and then the milk. He would then hand me the bowl and I was on my own to watch cartoons and eat cereal. I was at my happiest. Every now and then my mother would encourage me to stop waking up my father to ask if the cereal was ready. She wanted me to let him sleep and assured me that someone would fix the cereal when they woke up. My mother said when I was a little older I could fix it myself, but right now I was too little to pour the milk. Because of that, I'd just have to wait until an adult was awake (and willing) to fix the cereal.

That didn't sit well with me. I didn't want to disturb my father. He would have worked all night. I knew he was tired. All I knew was cereal was an important part of cartoon-watching. It was on this day that I decided the solution to all of this. I decided I didn't need milk. I decided it wasn't even necessary and it didn't even taste good. Without milk, I could fix my own cereal. On that day, I had my last taste of milk. I haven't had any since. Since that day, I have always eaten cereal right out of the box. My independence was born that day. I decided when the cereal was ready.

My Musings:

This was an important lesson about boundaries; not getting what you want because it inconveniences someone else. Although we're talking about cereal here, I was learning that sometimes even persistence doesn't work. Even when you want the most innocuous things if the person in power isn't up to granting it to you…you're out of luck. I was learning about power. I was learning quickly that people (even your father) weren't always interested in what you wanted and when you wanted it. It was here that I began to learn about developing alternatives. If my needs were not accommodated, I simply had to build an alternative. An alternative that was a win-win for all involved.

Your Musings:

_____

_____

_____

_____

Grade "A"

Being the child of an educator was an interesting experience for me. Almost everything I was involved in seemed to be about furthering my education. I was a bit of a loner and enjoyed playing alone in the playroom that my father created for me in the basement of our house. During the school year, my playroom was set up like a classroom (during the summer it became a house with miniature cooking appliances and the works). There was a black board in the front of the room and over 35 dolls perfectly lined up on shelves; in their proper position to be my "students." My mother even gave me a grade book where I recorded their grades each day. I taught, assigned homework, gave tests and even graded papers. Some of my dolls were white and some were Black. The white dolls seemed to get the best "grades." Many of my Black dolls and some of the less attractive-looking white dolls tended to get poorer grades. Though I was too young to understand it then, I was learning very early on about stereotypes, generalizations and prejudice; it was the beginning of the formation of my own implicit biases. I was taking my cues from society and my poor dolls took the brunt of it.

Over time, just like society, which was starting to become more integrated, there now were more Black dolls on the market. My mother began to buy more Black dolls for me. Mostly, this was because my Aunt Brenda, my mother's sister, refused to buy her daughter any more white dolls. She often proclaimed that Black people needed to buy things that reflected them. She was adamant that no daughter of hers would be walking around with a blue-eyed, blonde-haired doll. My mother began to follow suit. This dramatically changed the makeup of my "classroom." I guess I was experiencing the make-believe version of integration. Early on, the grading pattern didn't

change; the Black dolls still weren't doing as well. However, as my mother focused on increasing my number of Black dolls, I became acculturated to having them be a part of what I was doing. They became the norm. When that happened, the way that I felt about them – their value and their beauty – changed. All of a sudden, their grades improved. My Black dolls were smart and beautiful, too.

My Musings:
Societal issues became child's play during this time. The same way society reacted to race was also happening in my make-believe classroom. My idea of beauty and intelligence was being shaped at this young age. My application of societal beliefs played out in the grading system I created for my dolls. This was the making of implicit biases around race and attractiveness. Segregation in the broader society played out with me having all white dolls. When

my mother introduced the first Black dolls, I was lukewarm in my acceptance of them. Having Black dolls was not the norm, so my comfort level didn't shift until I got more Black dolls. I then began to normalize racial diversity in my make-believe classroom. I was also, unconsciously, learning that relationships and familiarity breeds acceptance. Without this, implicit biases remain alive and prominent in what we do each day.

Your Musings:

_____
_____
_____
_____
_____
_____
_____
_____
_____
_____
_____
_____
_____
_____
_____
_____
_____
_____
_____
_____
_____

Due Back Monday

When I wasn't playing school, I was doing something that was an extension of playing school. My parents sometimes forced me to go outside to play with the neighborhood kids. They recognized my joy was in my pretend world, but they knew how important it was for me to have social interactions and friendships. I was lucky enough to have great friendships in my neighborhood. All of us were about the same age. We were all about seven years old and even were in the same class at school. It was ideal.

I learned very quickly that even though we all lived in the same neighborhood, our lives weren't all the same. No one else had their own playroom like I did. I don't recall seeing the other neighborhood kids take long summer vacations away from Atlanta like we did. In some cases, I don't even remember seeing that the parents of some of my friends even work outside of the home. We were together…and different.

Sometimes, the kids would tease me and tell me "I had it made" because my mother was a teacher. They felt like I had an inside track of some sort. I guess in many ways I did. My parents were an early version of the Internet. If I didn't understand something, they either explained it or pointed me to the row of the always-up-to-date volumes of encyclopedia that we had on the book shelves. My mother had quite the collection of books in our basement. It was a wall to wall length shelving unit. I counted them once. There were over 600 books on those shelves. Sometimes, when I was playing school, I would take my dolls to the "library" (my mother's book shelves). Sometimes my dolls would stay at the library for hours (usually while I ate dinner or did my own homework). The collection was amazing.

During the summer months when my mother was out of

school for summer vacation from teaching, she always enrolled me in camp. Book Camp. Book Camp was like regular summer camp, except it centered around a library. She drove me there each day. The goal would be to read books and have group discussions about what we read. Each child would set a reading goal for the number of books they wanted to read by the end of the summer camp. My goal was to read 100 books. Each day I came home excited to tell my parents about either the book I had just finished or the book I had just started. They obliged me and though I'm sure they weren't the least bit interested in me explaining the capers of *Pippi Longstocking* or the adventures of *Betsy* novels, they always listened attentively and with awe of my accomplishments.

Book Camp seemed perfectly normal to me. I was not the least bit interested in tents, campfires or being outside, so this type of camp was perfect for a loner like me. I was in competition with myself to read 100 books. And you better believe, by the end of the summer I had read exactly 100 books.

What wasn't normal to me was the fact that none of my neighborhood friends were a part of Book Camp. When I asked if they were going I heard a range of everything from disinterest, to confusion about what a Book Camp was, to an interest but no parental support or even transportation in helping them get to the public library. This bothered me a great deal. Everyone should have been able to go to Book Camp. Reading was so much fun and it didn't seem fair that not everyone was doing it. Even my dolls were at the "library." Why weren't my friends?

It didn't take me long to determine that the answers to those questions might rest right in the basement of our own house. What if I created my own library; designed to support the kids in my neighborhood. They wouldn't have to worry about transportation or access. They could just come to our house and check out the books that they were interested in. I was so excited to be able to change the experiences of my neighborhood friends. They could now have a part of what I had. Their very own, accessible library.

This is where the work began. Although I was seven years old, I knew enough to know that to start a library I needed a strategy. I needed a check in and check out process. I needed a late fee strategy. I need a lost book fee. I even needed to decide when books were due to be returned. I decided to make it easy. All books would be **Due Back Monday**.

I was so excited to have a strategy and I went about implementation by taking a black permanent marker and writing Due Back Monday on all of the 600 books on my mother's book shelves. It didn't really matter what kind of book it was. The "D-E" encyclopedia was due back Monday. My mother's 1957 college yearbook was due back Monday. The original version of "Little Black Sambo" was due back Monday. I wrote those words large and boldly on the front cover of each book. It took me a couple of weeks to complete this first step, but I was proud.

I also made the check-out cards for the inside of each book. This allowed each person to write in their name and date of check-out; just like the cards at the real library. It also had the late fee (which was always 10 cents per day) and the cost of a lost book (which was a random dollar amount that I came up with for each book). About three weeks into the process, I was all done with setting my process. It was time to open the library.

I spread the news about my library by telling all of the neighborhood kids. They were so excited. I told them the hours of the library and they would just need to knock on the basement door. Kids in the neighborhood would come to check out books to read for leisure and even books that they needed to do homework for school. The library was working! The best part for me was that, inevitably, everyone was late bringing their books back. I was monitoring this and was more than happy to tell kids how much money they owed me. They had access and I was collecting fees, too. No one seemed to mind. A dime didn't seem to be a big deal. The kids also hadn't figured out that the best day to check out a book was Monday; if you did that you could keep it for a whole week.

My library went on for a few years. My mother added books. I was sure to write Due Back Monday on the front cover of those as well.

In 2001, the year my mother retired from teaching, she was sorting through some old books from the attic. She noticed that they all had Due Back Monday on the covers. She called me at my, now, home in Denver. I told her about started the library when I was seven years old. She was stunned. She had no idea I had been running a library from the basement of her house. I was almost 40 years old and she was just figuring out that social justice was happening right under her own roof! With her books (which, by the way, she began to scold me for writing on; 33 years too late).

My Musings:

I consider this experience the beginning of my social justice consciousness. It was during this time that I became intimately aware that not everyone had the same access to things. The broader society was teaching me in hard ways that Black and white people didn't have the same access, but this was different. I was learning that even Black people didn't have the same access as one another. As an only child at the time, I was also beginning to understand my privilege.

I had an abundance of many things I didn't have to share with anyone. This made it even clearer that I had plenty to give to others. I was acutely aware that there were systems that people couldn't access. In this case, the library. My parents were teaching me to be thankful for all that we had. That helped me to share with gratefulness and pride. I was learning at an early age that sharing assets increased the performance of the whole. In this case, creating a library for my community provided tools that everyone needed and appreciated. We all got better because of it.

Your Musings:

_____

_____

_____

_____

_____

_____

_____

_____

_____

_____

_____

_____

_____

_____

_____

_____

_____

_____

_____

_____

_____

_____

_____

_____

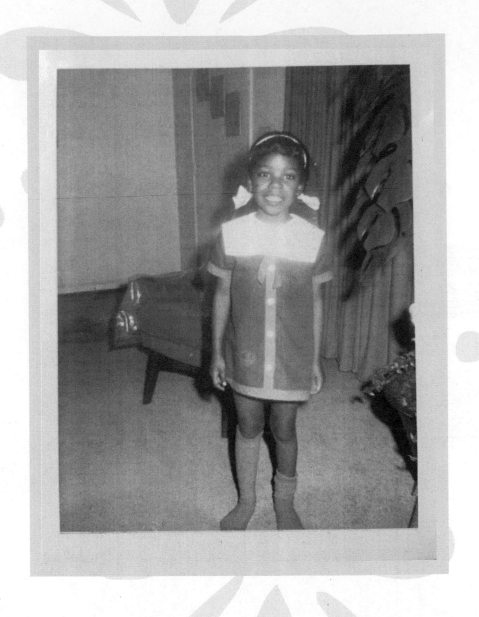

I See You

The best part of my neighborhood was the fact that almost every kid in the neighborhood liked each other. We played together each day, sometimes right in front of my house. We had very little traffic on our street, so it was not uncommon to see kickball or softball games happening right in the middle of the street. Everyone participated. If you didn't play ball, you were a cheerleader. If you weren't a cheerleader, you kept score. We are a fully engaged community of kids.

There was one kid that was a little different than the rest of us. His name was Clarence. Clarence was a little older than the rest of us. One of the adults in the neighborhood said he was 18. He didn't act like he was 18. He acted 9 or 10 years old like us; he was just a lot bigger. One of the neighborhood kids said he was retarded. I didn't know what that meant exactly, but I had heard some of the kids in our school special education class being called that. One of the kids said it meant they were stupid. That didn't sound good to me. Why would a person be born stupid?

I was really disturbed that Clarence, who hung out with the neighborhood kids each day, was being seen as stupid. He never really played games with us, but he was always a sideline participant or cheerleader in all that we did. He just wanted to be with us. Every now and then, one of the boys in the neighborhood would tease Clarence; agitating him so he would chase the group. I found it mean-spirited and often scolded the boys for teasing Clarence. Clarence seemed to like me. I was a little nervous around him. He drooled when he talked and that was disturbing to me. I couldn't understand why an 18-year-old presented in so many ways, like a baby. I didn't know any teenagers that behaved like him.

One time, Clarence rang our doorbell to see if I could come out to play. I am certain my father was concerned about Clarence's age as my playmate, but my parents used this as an opportunity to explain what mental retardation (or now, more appropriately, developmental delay/disability) meant. They explained to me that mental retardation didn't mean stupid. They encouraged me to challenge anyone who used that language to describe Clarence or anyone else with a disability. My parents said Clarence's brain wasn't developed in the same way as others and he needed extra help to understand. That sounded reasonable to me. If he needed extra help, we should simply help him. That is what we did with each other, so why would we behave differently when it involved Clarence? Mental retardation wasn't scary anymore. His brain was just different. How he moved in the world didn't match our way, but that was just fine.

My Musings:

Clarence represented my first foray into understanding people living with disabilities. I was introduced to negative language and stereotypes early on. It was an illustrative case of taking something we didn't understand (a person living with a developmental delay) and villainizing it in some way. Children were learning to make this disability scary so they could, quite literally, chase it away. This "chasing" was indicative of what happens when fear is present. When we are afraid, we tend to do irrational things to get the thing we are afraid of out of the way. It is the classic *flight or fight* syndrome. Some kids ran away from Clarence. Some kids chased and teased him into submission, so they could feel powerful over the very thing they were afraid of – his developmental delay. Were it not for my father explaining disabilities in such an empowering way I, too, may

have been relegated into the category of kids who saw disabilities as flaws and brokenness. It was at this point in my life that I was beginning to learn the power of our words, language and definitions. I learned that even one wrong word could negatively shape relationships and understanding for entire generations.

Your Musings:

_____
_____
_____
_____
_____
_____
_____
_____
_____
_____
_____
_____
_____
_____
_____
_____
_____
_____
_____
_____
_____

Camping in the City

Some of my fondest memories were spending the night at my grandmother's house. My younger cousin, Kim always spent the night with me. My grandmother lived in the city, on Hunter Street (what is now Martin Luther King, Jr. Drive) in Atlanta. My grandparents were the 2nd generation to live in their small 2-bedroom duplex. For me, being there was like Disneyland. I saw things I never saw living in the suburbs.

My grandparents lived on the 2nd story of the duplex and they had a large front porch that faced Hunter Street, the main drag. I loved the porch because you could see everything, but because of the beautiful flower boxes my grandmother had growing on the porch, no one could see you. It felt like we were in the woods; peering out into the jungle. It was our own secret garden.

My cousin Kim and I always considered our sleepovers at my grandmother's house, camping. We slept on her 2nd story porch a few weekends each month. My grandmother fixed all kinds of snacks for us to take on our "camping trip" on the porch. My grandmother felt comfortable with our camping. We were on the 2nd story and there was no way down from the porch. Kim and I felt comfortable, too, because our grandparents were right inside, close by.

My "camping trips" were my first insights into life, lifestyles and differences. I lived in the suburbs, so the sound of cars and ambulances and voices in the night was new to me. It was amazing that someone was always awake in the city. People were always walking, talking or yelling. Cars were always whizzing by. Ambulance sirens were constant. I loved hearing all of the sounds as Kim and I lay on a pallet on the porch. We would peer through the porch bannister late at night and we'd see the transsexual prostitutes walking the streets.

My grandfather told us they were really men wearing dresses. We'd giggle because we knew just enough to be dangerous about what a prostitute was. We found it even funnier that my grandfather said they were men wearing dresses. How could that be? Sometimes my cousin Kim would yell out at the prostitutes. I would hide because I didn't want to make them mad. My grandmother told me once that they were mean. They were men in dresses. They were mean. They were doing whatever prostitutes did; which I wasn't completely clear about. None of it made sense to me, but it was fun to see a life I didn't get to see at my house.

My grandfather was a weekend drinker earlier in his life. On some Friday nights, my cousin Kim and I would see him stumble down the street from an evening of drinking, headed toward the house. We would laugh at how drunk he was; swaying from side to side as he walked down the sidewalk. He was funny. It seemed like an eternity watching him come down the street and then waiting for him to climb the stairs to enter his house. When he finally made it in, we'd ask him for dollars. We knew he'd be too drunk to know if he was giving us $1 or $10. My cousin Kim and I made quite a bit of money off of my grandfather's inebriation on Friday nights. I figured we were making more money than the prostitutes were. All in the name of camping.

It was years later that I learned what **real** camping was. Tents, campers, the whole nine yards. I never heard of Black people doing it. All the images seemed to include white campers. Whatever the case, I assumed the way white people did it didn't result in the fun that we had watching my grandfather stagger down the street and seeing the prostitutes; men dressed liked women. I imagined the most excitement a white person would have camping was maybe seeing a bear. I'd take my drunken grandfather and the prostitutes any day!

My Musings:

This story highlights a myriad of things that I learned at a young age. The first thing I was learning about was the complexity of addiction. My grandfather was perfectly "normal" during the week; working each day as a member of the maintenance team at Georgia Tech. He worked hard and even sang in the church choir on Sunday. However, on Friday nights he was unrecognizable. His alcohol addiction was profound. Sometimes, I couldn't make sense of the differences in his behavior between Friday and the other six days of the week. My family remained silent about this behavior; almost minimizing it as if it weren't happening. I knew it was happening and I knew he was drunk. I began to believe that addiction was a choice and people could stop whenever they wanted to. It was the beginning of a new bias. One that gave me little capacity to understand the power that addiction had in the lives of others. Why couldn't everybody turn it off? My grandfather did every week. He was only an alcoholic on Friday's.

The other thing I was learning in this period was transphobia. My grandfather called the prostitutes "men wearing women's clothing." This was an absolute divergence from the societal standards that I knew about. Men did not wear women's clothes. Because of this, it was easy for me to see this as odd or wrong. This was complicated even more when my grandmother added that "these people were mean." It layered an already forming phobia with fear – the most dangerous combination of all. Interestingly, the notion of prostitution didn't scare me at all. The fear was around stereotypes of <u>who</u> the prostitutes were. Unconsciously, I was learning to fear people instead of fearing systems.

Your Musings:

_____

_____

_____

_____

_____

_____

_____

_____

_____

_____

_____

_____

_____

_____

_____

_____

_____

"

We need to normalize
the art of oral
storytelling (and the
documentation of it) in
a profound way as to
create other forms of
archives to preserve and
teach about our history.
From an equity lens,
many societal structures
have gotten in the way
of storytelling.

"

Are You Ready for your Close-up?

Growing up in the South presented many experiences that taught me about race, class, gender and economics. On one hand, I was a lucky girl that my parents took the time to educate me on just about every social factor you could think of. On the other hand, all of that knowledge about our world was making me a very angry child. I couldn't understand racism and every time I was presented with yet another example of it, I felt the anger grow inside me. My father was the best at calming me down and he explained how everything had a way of healing. That explanation worked when I was five years old. At age seven? Not so much.

I remember watching the news with my mother. It was a story about Duke University in North Carolina. The Afro-American Society students were leading a Black student takeover of a campus building to spark University action on the concerns of Black students. I remember looking at the images and thinking how ridiculous it was to have to do all of that to get attention from your school. My mother explained it as she had so many times before. She said, "they aren't interested in the concerns of Black people in this country."

That's it! I knew I had reached my limit. Enough was enough. Somehow, we needed a different strategy for ending all of this race stuff. Grown-ups clearly didn't know what they were doing and from the looks of it, neither did college students. I decided the best way to tackle this was to leave everyone behind and figure it out myself. I was going to run away from home.

As my parents were preparing for us to have dinner, I went to the front door. My father asked what I was doing. I told him I was running away from home. I told him grown-ups were too dumb to get the job done. I expected adversity, but instead I got a few moments of uncomfortable silence. Eventually my father spoke as my mother looked on with horror. My father said, "Wait right there a second. I need to grab my camera. I want to take a picture of you before you leave so I can always remember what you look like." The rest is history.

My Musings:

It was here that I learned about something called <u>The Power of the Pause</u>. I learned that sometimes there are sentinel moments in life that stop you in your tracks; keeping you from doing what you were setting out to do – even if what you were going to do was well-intentioned. These moments are divine in that they create just enough pause for you to make better decisions to get to the outcome you intended. In this case, my dad inserting a picture-taking pause made me think about the potential downsides to my running away. While I was pausing, I had a chance to think of other alternatives; making a way for new ideas. How often have you benefitted from The Power of the Pause? What are examples of times when things didn't go as well because of the absence of The Power of the Pause?

Your Musings:

_____

_____

_____

_____

_____

_____

_____

_____

_____

And the Emmy goes to...

Entrepreneurship was a big part of my childhood. I don't remember knowing any business owners, but there was something inside of me that always wanted to start something, run something or create something. I always wanted to fill gaps. I still do.

The library was just one example. Creating it was about providing access. I also noticed that outside of school field trips, the kids in my neighborhood also never got to experience the arts. My mother always took me to plays, the symphony and concerts. She even, God forbid, forced me to sing in the West Hunter Street Baptist Church choir. It was a historic church, pastored by the iconic Civil Rights giant, Rev. Dr. Ralph David Abernathy. What amazing exposure this created. To be in constant contact with Civil Rights giants was the norm for me. I knew, once again, my experience was different from that of the kids in my community.

I decided to bring the arts to my neighborhood. Each week, I would write a one-woman (well...one-girl) show to perform for the neighborhood kids. The show would include a play, a musical selection and a dance. Each week, a brand new show performed on our large backyard patio. Each week my father would help me set up the patio with chairs for the audience. He would sit inside the house in the large bay window and smile at me from above. I would charge a 10-cent admission fee and the neighborhood kids would pour in. They loved my plays. I played every role! The songs always involved a sing-along component. And, of course, I threw in some ballet or interpretative dance (with musical accompaniment by my father's portable cassette player). Each week I would receive a standing ovation and a whole lot of dimes. There was demand for the arts and I knew what I was doing mattered. Finally, my playmates had access to the arts, too. Even if it was me bringing it to them!

My Musings:

I was growing into my understanding of disparities during this point in my life. Even though we all lived in the same neighborhood, it was clear to me that we were not all experiencing the same things. The kids in my neighborhood weren't visiting the places my family visited. They were going to museums or plays or even the public library. What was normal at my house wasn't the norm at other houses on my street. I began to understand that I had access and privileges that other kids did not. Early on, this became a point of great contention in my spirit. I wanted everyone to have the same things; especially since we all looked the same. I'm not sure I was convinced (yet) that little Black children could have the same things as little white children, but I was certain that all little Black children should certainly have the same things as one another. My journey to create systems of equality began as intra-race endeavors. I wanted all of the other Black kids in my network to at least have the same opportunities I had. Equality shouldn't be that hard...should it?

Your Musings:

_____

_____

_____

_____

_____

_____

_____

_____

_____

Hot Diggity Dog!

Around age nine, I began to realize that not everyone in my neighborhood had exposure to dining out or restaurants. Most kids ate meals prepared by their mothers or grandmothers. We frequently dined out. My mother said it would teach us social graces; though she frequently said my father was a lost cause in this area. My father always winked at me because he knew my mother wasn't the greatest cook. Sometimes my parents would allow me to bring a friend along when we dined out. I could always tell that this was a very big deal for whoever we took. It was a big deal to me too, because I always wanted others to experience what I experienced.

I was especially close to two other girls in my neighborhood. They were each a year younger than I was, but we had so much in common. I shared with them a new business I had been pondering. A food delivery service. It would be like taking our neighbors out to a restaurant without them having to leave their home. My girlfriends loved the idea. We decided that we should sell hotdogs – plain hot dogs and chili dogs. We decided to charge 25 cents for the plain hot dogs and 50 cents for the chili dogs. We would take pre-orders and collect the money up front. We also decided that the orders would be delivered a week from the day we took the order. And so, it was! Off we went, knocking on every door of our neighborhood. Collecting quarters and raking in orders. It was amazing! We were rich. We had so many quarters we had to come to my house to unload them before we took more orders. At the end of the afternoon, we had taken orders for over 100 hot dogs. We hugged each other goodnight after a long afternoon of order-taking and then agreed to meet again the following afternoon to complete order-taking for the rest of the neighborhood.

After the second day of order-taking we had collected money for another 50 hotdogs. This was all unbelievable. Who knew it was so easy to get rich? I figured if we divided the money equally between us, we'd still be rich. Wow!

That night at dinner, I began to tell my parents about what me and my girlfriends had been up to over the past few days. It seemed the room went completely silent. My mother sat back in her chair with a look of disdain. She said, "you did what?" I repeated for her that we had taken prepaid orders for 150 hot dogs and chili dogs. I told her about the bags full of quarters we had collected. I was proud to tell her about the price differential between hot dogs and chili dogs and how much more we made just because of the chili. As I was describing everything, I noticed the biggest smile on my father's face, but it certainly didn't match the anger radiating from my mother. She made it a point to remind me that collecting money was not profit. She reminded me that we had missed two important parts of this strategy – the cost of the ingredients and the workers responsible for preparing the food. Who were the workers and who was buying all this stuff?

What started out as a proud moment suddenly turned into hell. We were less than one week away from the delivery date and I had no idea how we could pull this off. What I thought was wealth suddenly felt like a liability. I had no idea how much these ingredients would cost. Had we collected enough quarters? What was I going to tell my friends? Were we going to have to refund all those quarters? My mother was angry and I didn't know what to do. Later that evening I asked my father to help me to figure it out. He said his advice was to apologize to my mother and then simply ask for her help. That sounded so easy, but it was so hard to face my mistake. I was really great at being a visionary, but not so good at handling conflict. I followed my father's wise counsel and subsequently, my mother agreed to help me with the shopping and the preparation of the hotdogs. My girlfriends and I agreed to make all of the deliveries.

Delivery day came quickly. My mother had gathered a few of the neighborhood mothers to start the assembly line of hotdogs. I could tell she was still a little bitter, but she didn't let that get in the way of progress. As orders were ready, my girlfriends and I would check our list and deliver the hot dogs and chili dogs to the appropriate addresses. This wasn't so bad. The process was running smoothly. Until…

Until, the homes we delivered to wanted more hotdogs. They were so pleased with the hot dogs, they wanted more! Holy cow! What were we to do? That was easy. We accepted the money and took the additional orders. For every 20 hot dogs we delivered, there were 20 more orders. My mother couldn't figure out how we weren't keeping up with the orders. It got so hectic, one of the neighborhood moms had to go back to grocery store for more ingredients. To make matters worse (or better, depending on how you looked at it), neighbors then started ringing our doorbell to place more orders. My mother was clearly stunned! The orders were coming so fast, she didn't have time to be angry. Our house had turned into a fast food window. My dad pitched in and became a part of the "staff." It was marvelous chaos created by an entrepreneur with no financial plan. It is here that I learned that even equity is a business; with a cost and a strategy.

My Musings:

I don't even know where to start with this story! I would say I learned valuable life lessons about strategy and intent. This story taught me all about the importance of staying true to your real intent. I learned that any detour from pure intentions can lead to substantial hiccups along the way. In this story, I lost my focus on my pure intentions. My original intent was to provide equality and equity to everyone in my community. I wanted everyone to have equal access to something that they wanted or

needed. The intent was simple, pure and clear. The complication began when I clouded this pure intention with greed; I wanted to earn as many quarters as possible. The desire to earn quarters diluted my focus on community equity and equality and I lost my ability to even plan or forecast. What started as a great civic initiative was negatively impacted by over-focusing on the financial gain. We see this all too often in our communities. Good ideas clouded by over-focusing on financial gain. I learned that it is possible to be fiscally smart, financially successful and grounded in the principles of equity...all at the same time.

Your Musings:

_____

_____

_____

_____

_____

_____

_____

_____

_____

_____

_____

_____

_____

_____

_____

_____

"The topic of diversity has created the phenomenon 'diversity fatigue'. It means exactly what it says… people are tired of talking about diversity. We have either been talking about it for too long or we don't understand why it's such a big deal in the first place."

You Can Ring My Bell

At one part of my childhood, my father held a part time custodial job at a local mall. He would pick me up from school and bring me to the mall with him while he worked. I looked forward to this each and every day. My father would take me to the Walgreen's lunch counter first. He'd sit me up on the counter stool and I would tell the waitresses that I wanted "my usual." All of the waitresses were white, and they really loved me and my father. They got a kick out of me ordering "my usual" (which was a Coke and an order of fries). My father was introducing me to relationships with white people in a country that made this seem impossible. Every storeowner at this mall was white and they all seemed to love my father. I wondered how America be so screwed up while this mall was so perfect?

After finishing my Coke and fries, I said goodbye to the waitresses and hopped off the counter stool to go on my normal trek of visiting each storeowner in the mall. They all greeted me as if they hadn't seen me in weeks (even though they had seen me the day before). I visited the pet store, where I would eventually get my first poodle. I also visited a furniture store, where I believe I established my love and knowledge about mid-century modern furniture. During the holidays, I had a special friend. Her name was Madora. She was the woman who rang the bell for Salvation Army donations.

I was fascinated with Madora. She was a beautiful white woman in that very important-looking Salvation Army uniform. I was enamored with her bell and with the fact that people would give money to help other people. She smiled and when I'd walk up to her, she'd talk softly to me without missing a beat with her bell-ringing. When it wasn't Christmas, I had no idea where Madora went. I just looked forward to her coming back the next year. I assumed she might have been ringing her bell in some other part of the world. I hadn't figured out that Christmas was the same day almost everywhere in the world. I felt like I had a special, secret relationship with Madora. She told me she wasn't supposed to talk while she was working. I'd put a few pennies in the Salvation Army bucket and I'd whisper to her so no one would see us talking. Our secret was priceless to me. No one got to have a relationship with the Salvation Army lady but me.

The icing on the cake was one day, out of the blue, she handed me her bell and told me I could ring it for a while. I was in awe. I was standing beside Madora ringing the Salvation Army bell in the middle of the mall. I was proud and honored as I looked up at her smiling face. She was proud, too. I saw my father walk by as he was cleaning the mall. He smiled and I knew he was proud, too. I was doing important work with a woman I saw one month a year. I had grown to love her.

One evening, our doorbell rang. My mother commented that she wasn't expecting anyone. My father went to the door. To my surprise, there was Madora! She was standing in our living room holding the biggest stuffed animal I had ever seen. I ran to her and she embraced me. My father invited her to sit down and then Madora proceeded with telling me why she came to visit. Madora begin to explain to me that she wouldn't be ringing the bell any longer. She was getting married and was moving away. I felt like my heart dropped. I screamed "no" as the tears streamed down my face. I was losing someone I loved. Someone who risked her job for me. Someone who gave me a chance. My father orchestrated the whole visit. He thought it was important for Madora to talk to me directly. Today…I'm glad he did that. When I was a little girl, I felt it ripped the carpet right out from under me.

My Musings:

My journey with Madora was a great example of the impact that incremental steps can have on race relations and relationships in general. This "secret" relationship with Madora was a strong metaphor for what actually happens in race relationships. We don't wake up one morning completely woke; in complete understanding of one another. Our relationships are formed incrementally. We notice each other. We see the things that turn us on…or off. We maybe even take a risk. We share parts of our lives; even if the sharing is taboo or unexpected. Through these exercises, Madora and I developed a deep love for one another. She allowed me into her life and I allowed her into mine. Her actions extinguished the taboo nature of race relations of that time and opened the door to our hearts. Humanity became more important than societal discord or even our differences. The bell rang and we both answered.

Your Musings:

_____

_____

_____

_____

_____

_____

_____

_____

_____

_____

_____

_____

_____

_____

A Twisted Tale

Although I thought it was unfair that my parents would drop me off in Middletown, Ohio to visit with my paternal grandmother each summer, while they went on their "grown-up" vacation, I did like the many freedoms that I had there. My mother was the consummate Southern Belle and there were many things she didn't allow me to do, say or wear. In Middletown, my grandmother didn't know about these little nuances that my mother had, so I was free as a bird to live my life without my mother's boundaries.

One of the things my mother tended to be a stickler about was my hair and my clothes. She insisted I dress my age – 10 years old and she also had a strange rule about my hair. No braids or cornrows. This was always a point of contention for us. Cornrows and braids were a beautiful part of the Black community; braiding styles reflected our heritage and the amazing talents of local braiders. My mother would have no part of it. She would not allow me to have cornrows or braids. Each time I begged to have my hair braided, she would tell me "she wasn't going to have me looking like a pickaninny! A pickanniny? How on earth could my braids be likened to an image and language so derogatory? Why did I see cornrows as so beautiful, while my mother saw them as offensive and void of any culture at all? I settled into the fact that as long as my mother was in charge of me, I'd be forced to continue getting my hair straightened with that God-awful straightening comb; the one that nearly burned all of the skin off of each of my ears each time she used it on me.

When I was dropped off at my grandmother's house in Middletown, Ohio, I couldn't wait to catch up with my cousins and a few of my friends who were around my age. Each summer day was filled with adventure and fun. I loved it. On this particular day, my friend Carla said she was going to get her hair braided and invited me to come with her. I went excitedly, deep down inside wishing I could get my hair braided, too. The braiding shop was bustling with clients – each person sharing the kind of cornrow design they wanted. My friend Carla sat in the chair and began to get her hair braided. I was so envious. I didn't see anything pickaninny about this. The braider asked if I was going to get my hair braided. I hesitated in a way that almost took my breath away. I was in a position to make my own decision; even though I knew my mother would not approve. I thought for a minute, reassuring myself that my parents would be gone an entire month. That would give me plenty of time to enjoy my cornrows. "Yes!" I said. "I would like to get my hair braided." My friend Carla smiled and even gave me the money to get my hair done. As a loan. She said I had to pay her back.

After hours at the braiding shop, our hair was done. We were beautiful. I felt like an African Queen. Regal. I couldn't stop looking in the mirror at myself. My cornrows were in a pinwheel design. It was a piece of art. My friend Carla took pictures of my hair with her pocket camera. She said we'd rush to get the film developed so I could have the pictures forever as a reminder of how elegant I looked. When I got to my grandmother's house, I heard a squeal of excitement when my grandmother saw me. She thought my braids were beautiful. She said she had never seen that design before and made me model; turning to each side so she could check out the intricacies of the braid work. I looked forward to enjoying my braids all month. What a joy!

After about one week of relishing in the glory of my cornrows, there was an unexpected knock on the front door of my grandmother's house. I assumed it might have been my friend Carla or one of my grandmother's neighbors. But, it wasn't. I opened the door to find my parents standing on the other side of the door. Two and a half weeks early from the vacation. "Surprise!," they said. And surprised I was. I was coming face-to-face with my mother. The same mother who had absolutely forbidden me to have cornrows or braids of any type. The same mother who said being Black was hard enough; looking even blacker made life even more difficult. There we were.

My dad opened the door and embraced me as if he hadn't seen me in years. He said my hair was cool. He said I looked like an African queen. My mother glared at me and with a smirk, she said "you look like a pickaninny to me and you're not going back to Atlanta like that!" I was devastated. I could not understand why this was such a big deal to my mother. She was actually pretty mean about it. She actually hurt my feelings and she didn't seem to care about it. She seemed more focused on what other people would think of me because of my hair.

I was learning that straight hair was somehow better. Somehow prettier. Somehow whiter. My experience of being an African queen through my cornrows changed that day as my mother unbraided my hair. I didn't know how I could ever feel great about my hair again. Right there in Middletown, Ohio, my mother took my Africa out of me.

My Musings:

I could write a whole book about the plight of Black women and our hair. I'll save that one for later. I will say, that this story represents a scar that still plagues me today. I learned early on that my hair would define me in some way. My love for natural hair was extinguished at age 12 when my mother sent me to the hair salon for my first perm; designed to straighten the kinkiness right out of every strand of my hair. My mother was adamant that I would be judged by my hair, so the straighter the better. The more normal the better. This translated into "the more white-

looking the better." I remember grieving as my mother unbraided my cornrows. I felt like I was being robbed of something very important. I was developing a distaste for whoever these people were that didn't like my kinky hair. I felt pressure to maintain a look that wasn't mine. How could I be Black and proud and white at the same time?

Your Musings:

_____

_____

_____

_____

_____

_____

_____

_____

_____

_____

_____

_____

_____

_____

_____

_____

_____

_____

_____

_____

_____

_____

_____

" Equity shows up
in a variety of packages;
sometimes in
unexpected ways. "

Understanding Excellence

By the time I reached 5th grade, I was already in the category of "gifted and talented." I was reading at the 8th grade level in 5th grade and my parents had already been told along the way that the school wanted to have me skip grades. My parents refused. My mother, the teacher, said that was not a good idea. She said it had something to do with maturity. I had no idea what she meant by all of that.

I was a popular student. My teachers seemed to love me. They were so kind to me and the other students in the gifted and talented class (called the Enrichment Program). This new world was nothing like my 1st grade experience with Mrs. Brown. I wasn't sure if she even noticed I was smart. The Enrichment Program afforded me opportunities that the general student body didn't have. Special field trips and events. I even got a chance to be a legislative page in the Georgia State Legislature for Senator Pierre Howard. I didn't know who he was, but my family said it was an honor to serve. He later became the Lt. Governor for the State of Georgia.

I knew I was special and I loved these privileges. As much as I didn't like Mrs. Brown, maybe what she said about nincompoops was true. Maybe if you didn't act like one (whatever that meant), good things would happen. I was enjoying the privileges of not being a nincompoop and I liked it.

By the time I entered the classroom for 5th grade, I saw something I had never seen in elementary school. A Black teacher. Her name was Mrs. McFarland. She was a robust, regal and serious woman. Her presence filled the room. I think the first emotion, past being excited to see a teacher who looked like me, was fear. There was something about her that scared me a bit. She looked serious and I couldn't read if she liked me or not. She treated all of us the same – she certainly believed in equality. No one was special and we all got the same treatment and attention from her. My gifted and talented status didn't seem to matter to her. She expected excellence from all of us. I gathered quickly that she left little room for nincompoopness. I was petrified. My privilege was waning.

Mrs. McFarland was tough. She even questioned the validity of what I thought I was good at. Where I had experienced excellence, Mrs. McFarland determined, at best, it was average. I attempted to please her with my impeccable conduct. Mrs. McFarland remained focused on my academic performance; again, seeing some of it as mediocre. I was lost in my identity. Why was I stellar up to this point and now all of a sudden *average*? Clearly, the problem was Mrs. McFarland. I assumed she simply didn't like me. I even wondered if she knew what she was doing. I was sure this was true when I got my 5th grade report card and saw something I had never seen in my academic career. I had a "C" in language arts – the same area that earlier put me in the gifted and talented category. Why did Mrs. McFarland not understand I was gifted?

I established a dislike for Mrs. McFarland. Not because she was a bad teacher – she was brilliant. More because she didn't seem to understand that I was, in fact, very smart. I was angry each day and was beginning to lose my joy for school. I was even losing my joy for language arts. Even worse, I was losing my trust in teachers who looked just like me. Right about the time that I had written off Mrs. McFarland, our principal came into our classroom to tell us that Mrs. McFarland, who had been out sick for a while, had passed away. Our teacher was dead? How could that be. All of a sudden, my anger about receiving a "C" changed to sorrow. As mad as I was about my grade, it didn't matter as much as losing my teacher. I didn't get a chance to prove my worth to her. I realized she just wanted me to be great and she died pushing for it. I went to her funeral. My very first funeral. I looked into her beautiful white and pink casket and cried. I told her I was sorry for not giving her credit for being a great teacher. I hoped in some way she could hear me. I wasn't fair to her, but I did acknowledge that I was still a little angry. Maybe I wasn't the systems definition of gifted, but it was in that moment that I decided that to be gifted was about making her proud of me from that day on.

My Musings:

I didn't know it at the time, but I realize now that I was developing my new framework for success during this time. It was here that I was learning that white people weren't the only people I had to be concerned with. I was learning about the power of my Black elders; those trusted community figures that were there to hold you to a standard no one else could possible hold you to. Mrs. McFarland represented a presence in a system of education injustice that I had never seen before. She was my first Black grade school teacher. She respected each of us. She held us to an unwavering standard of excellence and she wouldn't back off. She chose her words carefully and she exposed us to the definition of empowering words; denouncing the notion that we were "less than" in any way. I begin to compare being called a nincompoop by my 1st grade teacher to now, being told I was gifted operating in a mediocre way. She really set the stage for me to live up to my destiny.

Your Musings:

_____

_____

_____

_____

_____

_____

Shiny Like Silver

My grandfather was fondly called "Honey" by all of the grandkids. I'm not sure why, but that is what we always called him. He wasn't a very educated man; only completing 3rd grade, but he was the nicest, kindest man you'd ever meet. He came from a family of mostly male siblings, but he did have a sister. We called her Aunt Bert.

Aunt Bert was very special. As a young girl, I idolized her. Except for the fact that she was Black, she reminded me of the moms on *Leave it to Beaver* or *Father Knows Best*. She was always dressed in high heels and pearls: even when she cooked. Her hair was always perfect. My grandmother said that was because it was a wig. Her house was beautiful. Everything looked like it couldn't be touched, like it was when my grandmother took me to Macy's and told me not to touch anything. Aunt Bert loved us, but she had no problem letting us know that she was a little different than we were.

One of the most memorable things about Aunt Bert was the amount of silver she had in her house. Everything was silver. The ashtrays, the candlesticks, the stems of the goblets and the serving platters — all silver. The vases, the napkin rings, the salad bowls — all silver. Everything was silver. My cousins and I used to pretend they were diamonds because everything was so shiny. Aunt Bert scolded us often, telling us that if we learned to behave and have class, we could be rich too. She said we would have to *"stop acting so Black."* Rich. Aunt Bert was rich. I guess I should have known with all of the silver and all. I learned quickly that she, like my 1st grade teacher, saw us as nincompoops. We weren't going to be rich because we were nincompoops. And, maybe too Black.

Years later. Aunt Bert passed away. She left a will and every piece of her silver was bequeathed to my mother. I'll never forget the day my mother found out that she was receiving all of the silver. I was excited. It meant we were going to be rich. Like Aunt Bert. I was stunned to hear my mother groan when she found out she was receiving all of Aunt Bert's riches. My mother said, "Oh Lord, who is going to clean all of that stuff? What a nightmare. Why did she leave me all of that stuff?" Was I hearing this correctly? Was my mother complaining about being rich?

My father, in his infinite wisdom, reminded me that we should be thankful for gifts. He also shared that receiving silver did not mean we were rich. It was here that I learned about how identity can be built around things. My Aunt Bert felt "better than" or "higher than" because of her bounty of silver; it defined her. In a world that had defined her negatively, she created an alternate world that covered her blackness with silver. Focusing on the silver helped her to not focus on her blackness.

My father taught me a valuable lesson that day. The day he was unpacking the sliver from boxes and polishing and placing it in the new curio he bought to hold it all. He said, "Baby, if all of your riches can fit in a box; you ain't rich." That moment changed the way I interpreted wealth and assets forever. True wealth is un-boxable! Richness doesn't involve a box.

My Musings:

It was here that I was learning that richness and wealth extended beyond material things. I still liked material things, but I was beginning to learn about other ways that wealth could show up. My parents were already teaching me about the power of education and community. This was the footprint for how I would later interpret what true power would look like. Later in my life, I recall the multitude of times when I, too, was packing

and unpacking or even losing boxes of "riches." My father was right. What was in those boxes were not an indication of richness. I now believe richness is a balance of being anchored in the expertise you have in your own lived experience, your engagement in a given community and your ability to be a part of a system of equity – one where you have everything you need to thrive.

Your Musings:

_____

_____

_____

_____

_____

_____

_____

_____

_____

_____

_____

_____

_____

_____

_____

_____

_____

_____

_____

_____

"

I'm not naïve. America wasn't built with equity in mind. It wasn't built with inclusion in mind. It wasn't built with equality in mind. Our country was designed to do exactly what it is doing. My thought is since we know what it was built to do, it might be time for a remodel.

"

Dilution

The next years of my life were filled with the typical teen-aged experiences: popularity contests, developing identities, growing and boys. I entered my freshman year at our neighborhood high school along with kids that I'd been with since 1st grade. We knew each other well. We even knew the upperclassmen because they, too, were kids in our neighborhood. It was nice to enter high school with some familiarity with those who were there. It made life easier for all of us. I felt secure.

I began to develop my new personality during my freshman year. It was a fresh start. Actually, the teachers gave all of us a bit of a break; they didn't know any of us unless they taught our older brothers or sisters. I didn't have an older sibling, so it was a great start for me. I had a chance to be "gifted" again. Or, so I thought.

Our high school had a racially diverse student body and faculty. This scared me a bit. I still had the Mrs. McFarland effect. I was still convinced I was cheated out of my gifted status and I was going to do everything to get it back. We had several Black teachers at our high school. I was already beginning to have a bias about their impact on me; even before I was assigned to their classrooms. I had already decided they wouldn't like me or understand my value. My go-to position was to avoid them at all costs. This worked just fine during my freshman year and my excellent grades proved it.

This was the point in my life that yet another set of biases were developing. I was learning that it was important to impress my white teachers and that my validation needed to come from them. I felt proud when they said I was smart or did well on an assignment. The more they validated me, the less I wanted interactions with teachers who were not white. When I did have interactions with the few teachers of color that I interacted with; I was less inclined to please them. The lack of racial diversity in the faculty made it easy to assume the few teachers of color had little power. I was beginning to learn what the white teachers wanted and then I'd do that; even it didn't make cultural sense for me and those students who looked like me. We saw the white teachers as the holders of power. Power. White power.

My Musings:

It was here that the realization of white supremacy began to manifest in negative ways in my consciousness. It was a complex time in American history and racism was institutionalized not just in systems and organizations, but was being normalized even in our thinking, I was determining who I needed to please. This was aligned with who I perceived to be the holders of power. To grow up needing this type of validation was a tragedy; a tragedy shared by almost every Black person I knew. It was almost like we needed a stamp of approval just to be whole. Just to be human. My personal biases were developing around who needed to validate my worth, who held power, who mattered. These were all negative traps in how I was formulating my thinking about myself, Black lives and what was needed for me to succeed in the world. My parents were working hard to combat this negative and prescribed way in which I was to think about myself and my blackness. They were soldiers in this work. I was slipping right into the structure of white supremacy. White people became the puppeteers for what I would do next. Or at least I thought so...

Your Musings:

_____

_____

_____

100

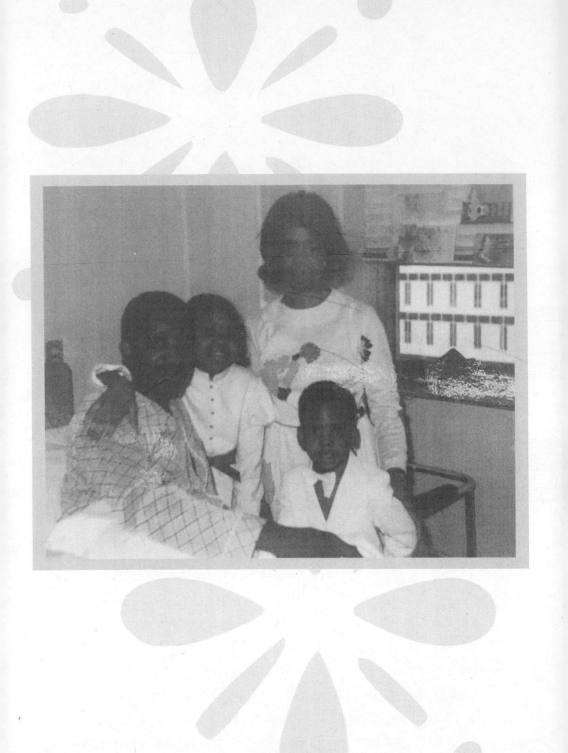

Mining a Metamorphosis

During the summer before my sophomore year of high school, two major things happened. My father had a massive heart attack. He was only 36 years old; a vibrant and strong employee on the assembly line at the local General Motors plant. His co-workers found him down and passed out on the assembly floor. They thought he was dead. He wasn't. He was just a 36-year-old man whose life was set to change forever.

The second thing that happened that summer was my parents put our house up for sale. They said it was time to get a larger home as I now had a younger sibling; my bouncing baby brother, John. I remember my father singing that theme song from the television show *The Jefferson's* "We're moving on up!" when he described why we were moving. I could tell my mother wasn't too keen on any of it. She really liked things to stay the same. I don't think I even paid attention to this moving process. People came by to look at the house. I never really saw myself anywhere else, so the presence of potential buyers went right over my head. I was just as content as my mother. Content...or maybe even naïve.

My father's heart attack was so massive; he was forced to retire on permanent disability. I didn't realize the gravity of retirement on his young life, but I knew that he would be home with us at night and would be able to spend more time with us during the day because he wouldn't be at work. This sounded exciting to me.

While he was still hospitalized for his heart attack my father insisted that my mother continue to shop for our new house. I thought this was silly since our current house hadn't sold. My mother would show him pictures in this massive real estate book of the houses the realtor was showing her. We'd sit on the hospital bed with my father and he'd smile as my mother flipped the pages to houses in neighborhoods I had never even heard of. Our realtor was a larger-than-life white man named Dewey. He seemed genuinely interested in helping us. Funny. He kind of reminded me of Miss Ann; the white ballet teacher who came to teach Black girls to dance. Mr. Dewey seemed to be helping us to learn about a world that was bigger than the one we knew about. Somehow, it seemed risky for him to be doing this, but he did anyway. I was smart enough to know that he was really interested in exposing us to a fairly white world.

On this particular Sunday, while visiting my father in the hospital, Dewey dropped by with some news. Our house had sold. It was time to make an offer on our favorite house. Seemed easy enough. I had gone with my mother to many of these unknown neighborhoods on the far outskirts of Decatur, Georgia. A place, during this time, where there was little going on in the area. Sizeable homes and good schools and mostly white communities.

We picked our favorite house there. We toured it once again and I even remember journaling a description of every detail of the house; from the beautiful shower curtains to the English Tudor design of the house. I read what I had journaled, so my father would get the full effect of the house from his hospital bed. It was all very magical and my father said my mother and I should make the offer. We did. Mr. Dewey called the owners from the hospital and they accepted the offer the same day. Just like that…our lives had changed forever – from my father's hospital bed.

My Musings:

This story is the catalyst of great changes in the world and in my life. I didn't know at the time, but this would be a poignant example of the complicated elements of housing integration. The juxtaposition of my father's premature retirement and a substantial move to a new community would become life

changing for all of us. As much as we were coming out of severe and historical racial trauma; from housing, to education to experiences, this move would bring about even more complexities. I was revisiting what I learned about being rich. I felt we were entering into a "richness" I had never experienced. My father's retirement allowing him to be home each day. Our new house. Our new furniture. Even our white neighbors. We had arrived. Or had we?

Your Musings:

_____

_____

_____

_____

_____

_____

_____

_____

_____

_____

_____

_____

_____

_____

_____

_____

_____

_____

Moving Mountains

My father's recuperation was a lengthy one. Over 50% of his heart had been compromised, so he had to take it easy. The new owners of our house were pressing for a quick move-out day and my father was still in the hospital. My mother, a creature of contentment, was in denial about the urgency of our move-out date. She made no preparations. Dewey, our realtor, shared with my father that we had to get the plans in place to move. My father told him not to worry. He'd handle it.

Two days after this conversation with Dewey and having spent almost three weeks in the hospital, my father was being released. My mother went to work as usual this day. She had not gotten the message that my father was being released that morning. I recall being home (it was a teacher's planning day, so we were out of school) when my father walked in the front door of our now, sold, house. I was so excited to have him home. It was like he had been gone for years. Before I could curl up on the couch to talk to him as I loved to do, he looked at me and said, "we've got work to do – we have to move today."

Move? Today? The same day he got home from the hospital? Yes. That is what he meant. And that is what he facilitated. Within an hour, our house was filled with men. Some I knew and others I had never seen before. All of them working feverishly to get every room packed and moved to our new house. Right before my eyes, my whole 14-year-old life was disappearing as each room was emptied out in warp speed. I couldn't catch my breath. My past and my future were intersecting too fast. I felt like I couldn't grieve; I couldn't say good-bye. There was no time for emotion. My father was also facilitating the movers bringing things into the new house. At certain points, he was at the old house while I was telling them where to place things in the new house. My father had given me the awesome responsibility to design the look of our new home. I was proud. I was like an air traffic controller, telling the movers where everything should go. It took the sting out of the gravity of this moment.

Around 3:45 pm, when my mother finished her teaching job for the day, she came home. The old home. She was stunned when she walked in and saw my father standing there; released from the hospital without her knowledge or help. She was even more stunned (and frankly, angry) when she looked past him and saw that the contents of the entire house were gone. I saw her cry. All I knew was there was no time for grief. We had a new house. A new life. A new community. And it was all starting right now.

My Musings:

It was here that I began to learn about the importance and power of being anchored in what you are familiar with. My whole life up to that point had been spent with the same kids, same families and same community. I learned valuable life lessons in this community. We knew each other well and we were, indeed, the village that loved each other. Literally, overnight, my father dismantled what we knew best. He was removing us from what we were most familiar with; leaving no time for processing what was happening in our lives. We were moving in the name of progress and success; leaving our souls behind. There was no conversation about the beauty and memories of what we were leaving. There was also no substantive conversation about what we were moving into. All I knew was we were successful and that was supposed to be a good thing. All I felt was a panicked hope.

Your Musings:

Game On

My father and I privately chuckled about how mad my mother was when she came home from school and her old house was gone. It all happened so fast, I don't remember if she ever even had time for proper goodbyes with the old neighbors. All I knew was we were gone. We had a beautiful home and our lives seemed charmed.

My maternal grandparents were so proud of my parents. They congratulated my parents on this big accomplishment and the pride they had lit up their faces when they came into the house. My paternal grandmother on the other hand, didn't feel quite the same. She had flown in from Ohio a few days prior to my father being released from the hospital. She was horrified that he was moving our house on his first day home. Somehow, she blamed my mother. She told people back in Middletown that my father did all of this because "my mother wanted it – she wanted a new house and she wanted it now!" I knew this wasn't true. My mother didn't know any of this was happening and could have frankly lived at our old house for the rest of her life. However, my grandmother spent the rest of her life believing my father was pressured to move into our new house; this new world, while severely ill.

My Musings:

I was learning very quickly about pride and accomplishment. My grandmothers appeared polarized on the issue of our family progress. One grandmother beamed with pride that we had moved out of our old community into this new (and white) neighborhood. The other grandmother seemed to think my father was being forced to go to this unknown land of white people. It was fascinating to see, even in the very same family,

how one elder saw progress and the other saw advancement under duress. I learned to balance my perspectives; always wondering, however, which one was true. Did we move to this white community because of progress and new power or were we here because we had a point to prove? Black people belonged here, too.

Your Musings:

_____

_____

_____

_____

_____

_____

_____

_____

_____

_____

_____

_____

_____

_____

_____

_____

_____

_____

_____

_____

"

Calling out culturally destructive behavior should not always be on the shoulders of minorities. Everyone has a responsibility to create a safe and inclusive environment.

"

Oteal Bowen

The Shotgun Effect

Our first night in the neighborhood was so quiet it was almost deafening. There were no voices of children playing in the streets. Just silence. I convinced myself that this was temporary and the sounds of laughter and joy would come later. My mother said white people probably didn't play in the streets. I found this strange, but so far, it looked like she may have been right. I didn't see a trace of kickball games or jump rope in our streets. Just people taking walks and looking over at our house when they walked by. Our next-door neighbors, both white families, seemed to be very nice. They waved and smiled and over time the housewives got to know my father well because he, too, was home all day – except he was there learning to be retired and disabled.

When we woke up on Saturday morning, my family was horrified to see that our front lawn had been vandalized. Our trees had been draped in toilet paper, eggs were thrown all over the front of the house and our mailbox had been knocked down. It was a complete mess and somehow it had all occurred while we were sleeping. My parents were strangely silent. They had to be mad. Our beautiful home was terrorized. The only house in the neighborhood to have had this happen. Why us? Why our house?

My father finally spoke. He said, "they don't want Black people in this neighborhood." The words paralyzed me. Why on earth would we move to a place where they hated us? I thought we were done with all of that. My maternal grandmother told me how far we had come in the Civil Rights Movement. It was one of the reasons she was so proud of my parents buying a house here – in this white community. It illustrated equality and justice for them. In that moment, it illustrated a headache to me. I knew, in that moment, that I had to put up with being looked down upon even when equality was present. Our house was just as nice, just as big and just as expensive as those of our white neighbors and they still thought we didn't belong there. Why didn't we simply stay at our old house?

From that day forward, my father would wait until my brother and I would go to bed and he would go and sit on the front porch, in the dark, so no one could see him. I only knew this because my mother secretly told me he was on night watch – guarding the house from vandals. Guarding the house from vandals? This was 1977, not the Civil War! I couldn't believe it. One night I tip-toed downstairs to take a look at him doing this. There he was, just like my mother said. In the dark on the front porch. Holding a shot gun. Where did he get a shot gun and what was he going to do with it? The last thing we needed was for my father to shoot vandals. My God! Why didn't we stay at the old house? My father was being provoked to shoot at people who threw eggs at our house. This white community thing was feeling stranger by the minute.

My Musings:

As happy as I was to experience the new "riches" of living in our new house, I was deeply troubled by the behavior of our neighbors and even the new behavior of my father. I had never seen my father in a defensive posture like this. He was normally the peacemaker; the one focused on social justice in such a beautiful, collaborative way. To see him on our porch with a shotgun (even though I learned later it was an empty chamber and he didn't even own bullets) was horrifying. I was beginning to question if progress was worth it. Why was it so important to be the Black family in the white neighborhood? Why did we need to fight for our existence in a plain, ordinary subdivision? We owned our home just like everyone else in the neighborhood. What was missing was the village; a community that loved each other through the hard times.

Your Musings:

School Daze

Entering a new high school was harder than I thought. Gone were the familiar faces of kids I grew up with. I had entered a predominately white school; with the exception of the Black kids who had been bussed there. I learned very quickly that the white kids wanted to know right up front if you were one of the "bused in kids" or one of the kids who "lived in the neighborhood." I found, over time, that it had become important to delineate which one I was. Even if they didn't ask. There was a real class system developing. Somehow, the kids who were bussed in from other communities were looked down upon – like they didn't belong there. The neighborhood Black kids were received well. We had some strange kind of privilege. The privilege of being a part of this white group.

There were a few Black faces on faculty – mostly coaches or health education teachers. The bused Black kids stayed together; isolated in many cases from us. It didn't take me long to realize the Black kids were a bit of a clique – there were so few of us, we got to know each other quickly and intimately. I liked this. I enjoyed meeting the Black kids that lived in my community. Our neighborhoods seemed so vast and isolated and seeing us all together at school brought a bit more intimacy. I asked my new friends if their fathers had to sit on their porches in the dark with a shot gun. I got casual laughter and no real answers. I knew then that our house being vandalized had not been an isolated event. I also knew our Black "privilege" silenced our desire to talk about race, racism or shot guns.

My Musings:
I was learning about intra-race dynamics during this period. These dynamics were fueled by the construct of white supremacy,

but nevertheless, it is something to explore. The division between (1) Black kids that were a part of our school due to busing and (2) Black kids that were there because their families had integrated these predominately white communities was extraordinary. We were taking our queues from what white kids were saying. They had stratified the bused kids as those kids coming from the bad, dangerous schools. The "bad, dangerous" schools were almost exclusively schools that were predominately Black. It was the established code words for schools that weren't white. Black students who lived in the neighborhood wanted to be sure they weren't seen in the same light as the bused kids. I saw us making it a point to do things like share what street we lived on so the white kids would know we were their neighbors. Even sadder, we didn't socialize much with the bused in Black kids. We were learning and developing explicit biases; biases we thought were helping us to be more accepted in a world that didn't accept us anyway.

Your Musings:

_____

_____

_____

_____

_____

_____

_____

_____

_____

_____

_____

"
Equity is
systems change.
You could do
diversity and
inclusion work
and never actually
impact systems.
"

White People Really Love Salad

After about six months in our new neighborhood and becoming more familiar with classmates who lived right there on my street, I was invited to have dinner with one of my white classmates. She lived around the corner from our house. I was a bit nervous because I had never eaten dinner at a white person's house before. My father said it was no big deal. He said, "they have the same kind of forks and knives that we do." He always knew exactly what to say. My mother grimaced.

I went over for dinner and my classmate, Jen, was just as fun and cheerful as she was in school. Her mother and father introduced themselves and welcomed me to the neighborhood. My friend showed me around their house. It was funny to see how much it looked just like our house. Before we sat down for dinner, Jen's parents invited me into the den to chat. They were very nice but asked me a lot of questions. They wanted to know what my parents did for a living. They wanted to know where we moved from. They even asked me if my parents went to college. I thought there were too many questions, but I answered them anyway. I wondered why they didn't save the questions for my parents. I figured they were just getting to know us better. My mother would have considered the questioning a sign of just being nosey. I would understand later that it was a sign of our white neighbors trying to qualify how we ended up in the same class system with them.

Dinner was served in the formal dining room. I felt special. We normally only used our formal dining room for holidays or very special dinners. As I sat down at the table next to my friend Jen, her father began to pass the salad bowl around the table. I had just a tiny serving of salad. I wanted to save room for the entrée. I was astounded by the large amount of salad that each of them put on their plates. Their salad took up the whole plate! I kept wondering how they would ever have room for the rest of the dinner items. I decided white people really loved salad.

After the salad and a lot of conversation, I waited for the next course. It never came. Horrified, I soon realized that the salad was the dinner. I was dumb-founded! What was going on here? Why didn't Jen's family have food? The evening wrapped up with an after dinner warm apple cider, more "nosey" conversation and then I walked home.

When I got home, my parents eagerly asked me to tell them all about my dinner experience at Jen's house. Solemnly, I told them it was really pretty sad. I shared that Jen's family was poor and they could only afford to have salad for dinner. My mother was stunned. "Just salad?" she said. "Yes," I answered. "Nothing else?" my mother asked. "Nope, just salad," I shared. My parents couldn't believe it. We had moved to this white neighborhood, had our house vandalized, had been looked down upon and there on the same street were white people that didn't even have food? My father said he couldn't figure out why people would live in a nice neighborhood and have nothing in their refrigerator. I agreed. My mother used his comment as an opportunity to remind my father that sometimes you just needed to be content with living in your old circumstances instead of keeping up with the Joneses. My father rolled his eyes and proceeded with trying to figure out how to help Jen's family.

At the end of the week, my parents told me they had come up with a plan to help Jen's family. My mother was going to make a big meal and we were going to take it to their house. My father said it was kind of a *reverse welcome wagon* – the new family brings something for the old family. I loved the idea. God, my father was brilliant! My mother spent all day making everything from macaroni & cheese, fried cabbage, fried chicken to peach cobbler and pineapple upside down cake. It was a feast and there wasn't a salad in sight.

I called Jen and asked if we could swing by for five minutes; my parents had a surprise for them. She was excited and her parents welcomed us. We packed up the food and loaded it in our car to drive around the corner to Jen's house. It was too much to carry. We rang the doorbell and Jen's father answered. He and my father met and shook hands.

My father said, "We wanted to share my wife's great cooking with you. We made way too much for ourselves and thought you might enjoy it." I stood stunned for a minute. We didn't make way too much for ourselves. My mother made the food because these white people were poor. They only had salad and needed some food. Jen's family seemed so excited to receive the food. It was sort of sad. I hoped that would be the last time they would have to eat just salad for dinner.

My Musings:

As funny as the story is now, it was a great example of how not understanding cultural norms can lead to stereotypes and generalizations. Even the most obscure things (like salad as an entrée) can kick-start next steps that might be unnecessary and ill-informed. Not understanding cultural norms and practices of other groups forces us to apply our own standards and norms in order to make sense of what we're seeing and experiencing. You see, in my Black experience, salad was rarely a part of the meal and in the rare occasions that it was, it was served as a small side dish. Seeing it as a main course represented scarcity; the absence of "real food." Applying my own norms and practices to this scenario forced me to see this family in a deficit position. This happens in all kinds of scenarios. Unchecked, this can become the basis of racism and all kinds of "othering." If what we see doesn't look, feel, taste, or sound like what we know best...

something must be missing or wrong. This ideology keeps us from fully understanding and participating in the lived experiences of others. I truly believe relationship building is an important factor in eradicating almost any form of discrimination we have. If we don't know each other, we won't get each other.

Your Musings:

_____

_____

_____

_____

_____

_____

_____

_____

_____

_____

_____

_____

_____

_____

_____

_____

_____

_____

_____

"
Oftentimes, this
work may seem
revolutionary
because we feel
frustrated and we
know that changes
need to be made
now. But the
reality is equity is
evolutionary work.
"

And the Winner Is...

As I moved through my teens, my mother began urging me to work on my shyness. She counseled me to get involved in school activities. I was in the band, but she said this wasn't enough. She said broadening my activities would help my confidence. I was relatively shy and pretty insecure. I spent a lot of time comparing myself to other girls in my school; most of whom were white, blonde and equipped with boobs (which were noticeably missing on me). I felt like the flat-chested little Black girl in a sea of white, blonde bombshells. It was right about then that I began to question my beauty and my negative thoughts about my body image intensified. I just couldn't measure up to these white images. My hair wasn't the same. My body wasn't the same. Nothing was the same. The skin I was in simply didn't fit in.

When I came home from school on this particular day my mother was excited to share a letter with me. It was from one of those Miss Teen pageants in Atlanta. She had requested the information and an entrance application. She said it would be a great opportunity to build my confidence by competing. I was horrified. Why would I want to be in a beauty pageant? My mother was persistent. Long story short…she helped me with my entrance application and I was accepted as a contestant. My mother was convinced this was the right pageant because it had a strong oratory and writing component – there was an essay competition. Unlike my 5th grade teacher, my mother saw this as my strong suit. She saw this opportunity as a way to strengthen my confidence by learning to speak in front of large audiences.

I kept my involvement a complete secret from my friends. I wasn't pretty enough to be in a pageant, so I didn't want the uncomfortable task of having to explain how I even got in. No one had ever heard of getting in a pageant to learn how to be a speaker, so sharing that would have been ridiculous. I just went along with my mother and moved through the process of quietly preparing for this pageant.

On our pageant orientation day, I learned that there were about 50 other contestants. I also felt the blood drain out of my face when I realized that almost 49 of them were blonde bombshells. Though we were all about the same age, they looked so mature and… well, developed. At 15, I looked like a 6th grader in this sea of very developed white girls. I was doomed. How did I let my mother get me into this mess?

The pageant director came in and advised us of all of the responsibilities we would have as contestants in this pageant: evening gown competition, essay competitions and volunteerism responsibilities. All of it sounded scary to me and all I could think of at the moment was how my 6th-grade looking body would stack up against the other 49 contestants in an evening gown competition. It was like Barbie versus Skipper. Or Marcia Brady versus Jan Brady. It was just no comparison. When I got home that night, I cried harder than I had ever cried. I told my father that I was tired of Black people always being in a position of losing. I told him that I knew I had lost the minute I walked in the room with all those contestants. He was silent for a moment and then he said, "Trust me. You've already won. You just don't know *what* you've won yet. Sometimes the prize isn't what you think it is."

My Musings:

During this period, I was coming face to face with America's model of beauty and it was clear that it didn't include anyone that looked like me. Everywhere I looked, I was the anomaly. My mother assured me that I looked exactly the way a 15 year

130

old girl should look, but when I looked around at the other 15 years olds – the white girls – well, I didn't stack up. Literally. They looked like the women on television. The actresses. The models. They were confident and developed. Less girl, more woman. It was a standard that I didn't have access to. Whenever I looked at beauty pageants or flipped through teen magazines, all I saw was the image of mature white girls. When would I see a picture of someone who looked like me? As much as I was living through the era of "Black is Beautiful," I was learning that the mainstream media didn't seem to think so. We weren't glamorized on television or in print and the only time I saw our beauty was in Black magazines like *Ebony* or *Jet*. All of this was keeping me from visualizing excellence. How could I compete or even match these standards that America was setting? These standards that a Black girl could never achieve. I was learning about fatalism and defeatism at a young age.

Your Musings:

_____

_____

_____

_____

_____

_____

_____

_____

_____

_____

_____

_____

_____

What's Right About America?

Preparing for the oratory competition was beginning to be fun. We had all learned that the title of the speech we had to write was "What's Right About America." I was intrigued by the title because I knew, as a Black girl, I could share some perspectives that the other contestants could probably not. The topic forced me to see "right" in a world that had been so "wrong." I spent weeks with the door closed in my bedroom working on my speech. Finally, I had it. I determined what was right about America in 250 words or less and I was ready to tell the world. I practiced delivering my speech to my parents each day. Each time, my father said it was the best speech he had ever heard. Each time, my mother corrected my diction or told me to hold my head up. I went through the trauma of being fitted for a special "What's Right About America" costume for the competition. It was horrifying. I had to wear shorts; showing my ultra-thin, Olive Oyl-like legs. I was back in my body image insecurities and was losing my focus on my speech. I begged my mother to have them redesign my costume to cover my legs. She said I was being over dramatic. She reminded me that Twiggy was a famous star because she was skinny. That piece of information didn't help me one single bit. Who in the heck was Twiggy?

The day of the pageant was a strange mix of excitement and fear. It was a culmination of several months of practicing, camaraderie and civic engagement. I even had an opportunity to volunteer at the Scottish Rite Children's Hospital, where I sat and talked to a very sick paraplegic Black girl who I was told would spend the rest of her life there at the hospital. I felt grown-up when I went to sit with her each week. She made all of my insecurities go away and she taught me about body image. She was older than me and was missing parts of her body. She still wanted her hair to be pretty and she seemed to have a self-esteem that I couldn't understand. I brushed her hair each time I visited. She told me beauty came from within. She was right. She was the most beautiful girl that I ever met. She told me winning the pageant wasn't the point; being in the pageant was the point. I've never forgotten her. She died one week after the pageant. She changed my life.

I ended up making the Top-5 in the essay competition, so I (along with four other contestants) were going to be delivering our speeches in front of the hundreds of people sitting in the audience. It was a surreal moment to step onto the stage. A big moment for a shy, Black girl in a country that couldn't even see her.

The night of the pageant, I was as insecure as a girl could be. I was certainly proud to be in the top five for the essay competition, but somehow that didn't make up for how I felt about myself. I was still fixated on seeing myself as less than others; kind of like I treated my Black dolls in the days that I played school in my basement "classroom." I went back to my elementary school days when I went from "gifted" to "average" in the eyes of one teacher. I remembered being called a nincompoop and how that definition might just be true. As I got dressed in that competition costume that accentuated the essence of my skinniness, I looked in the mirror and remembered a promise I made. To a woman who lay in her casket. I promised Mrs. McFarland that I would make her proud.

My speech created a silence in the room. You could hear a pin drop. It appeared the audience was mesmerized by both my honesty and my thoughtfulness in describing how something so complicated like race in America, could catapult us all into healing as a country. Like magic, my words felt much older than I was. I felt like I wasn't in control of my delivery or what impact it was making on others. All I know is that I finished. The crowd rose to its feet in applause and I stood in absolute amazement. I did it. I described what was right about America while standing in everything that was wrong in America. That night I learned that what is right and what is wrong live together. That night I also won 1st place in the oratory component of the pageant.

My Musings:

It was here that I began to learn about my voice. Most of my childhood had been spent focusing on my brain – my grades, my academic achievements. Now I was in a period of taking my deep thoughts, experiences and insights and using my voice to share them. I realized during this period that internal pain could easily become power. I began to remember the things my parents shared with me along the way. They always reminded me that I didn't have to cave in to being defined by others even though the color of my skin was causing that to happen on a larger level. They told me to never let a flaw in the system stop me. They explained this as a systems issue. They said it wasn't personal because they didn't want me to go through life being mad at people. My father always said, "be mad at the system and go fix that!" That advice has dramatically shaped how I do my work in the areas of diversity, equity and inclusion. It was here that I learned to draw out power during oppression. Love during hate. Rationale out of chaos.

Your Musings:

_____

_____

_____

_____

_____

_____

Chasing the Football

Going off to college was easy. I didn't have a choice. My parents said I was going and I just needed to determine, within reason, where I wanted to go. I was a big football fan and secretly, I wanted to go to the school that had the best football team. I told my parents that I was looking for a good academic system; my father knew fool well that I was following the football. I chose the University of Alabama in Tuscaloosa, Alabama. National champions, only three hours from home and a chance to be in the marching band. I won't deny that they also had a strong academic system. It couldn't have been more perfect.

At my off-to-college going away party, my family and friends gathered to wish me luck and a fond farewell. My maternal grandfather, who I loved for his less-than-tactful-delivery, reminded me "not to get too big for my britches by coming home with a white boyfriend." I was horrified that he said this out loud in front of all of the guests and I remember the grimace my grandmother gave him. We wrote it off as his concern for me, but I'd come to realize later he was on to something.

I was proud to enter the University of Alabama. I walked onto the campus and breathed in all of the regality of it all. It was famous and historic, and the football team was like none other. I was in the band and would be traveling with the team. My beginning couldn't have been better. My parents drove up to my new dorm; an older dorm that housed mostly freshman girls. I would be sharing a room with someone named Lisa. I got to the room first and begin to unload and decorate my side of the room. My mother had impeccable taste, so my décor was just like home. I imagined my room winning the prize for "the dorm room that looked least like a dorm room."

A few hours later, my roommate Lisa arrived. She was white. Her parents were polite and greeted me and my parents. They looked around the room, made some small talk with us and with each other and left. I assumed they were going out to dinner or a tour of the campus. My parents and I were going to do the same thing. I was wrong. Lisa never came back. I heard her parents decided she would move to a different room. I never heard why. I saw Lisa a few days later. In my same dorm. With her new roommate. A white girl named Elizabeth.

College was a tremendous learning experience for me. I learned quickly that white students knew about a thing called networking. They had different relationships with teachers than I had ever seen. Some of them even had lunch meetings with professors. I learned the white students came from generations of people who went to the University. Their parents knew the professors and the people in the front office. College seemed easier for them. The relationships seemed easier and the white kids seemed more practiced in asking for what they wanted…and getting it.

The first year of college was my year of freedom. I was experiencing my first time away of home and going to class wasn't an integral part of it. I was not being my best. Mrs. McFarland, my 5th grade teacher, would not have been proud. I was wasting resources and time trying to be an adult. There was nothing gifted about what I was doing. I was, however, doing what I saw other students doing. However, I didn't realize that being "networked" could get you through mediocrity. As I entered into my foray of being placed on Academic Probation during my freshman year, my father promptly drove 3 hours from Atlanta to tell me if he ever saw grades like that again, I would be brought home to attend community college. From that point forward, I had good grades, even graduating on the Dean's List. I also learned that privilege was a real thing. It got some through…while leaving others behind.

After graduating from the University of Alabama, my career progressed in important ways. I married my college sweetheart (we later had our daughter, Jasmine, and also eventually got divorced). I didn't have the benefit of being networked or coming from a family that was a part of a legacy of any corporation. I just showed up to each company that I worked for, with all of my kindergarten through college finesse each time. Each time provided a more powerful, albeit not perfect, experience than the last one. It is here that I began to see the relevance of my upbringing and my stories as I began to unravel equity and what it would take to design a world of systems where everyone could thrive.

My Musings:

As equipped as I felt to go to college, I learned quickly that race was still an issue in America. My college experience began with racial hurt. I was catapulted into feeling "less than" very quickly. I wasn't even good enough to be a roommate to a white person. The tide was rolling and not in a good way. I also remembered the words of my grandfather before I headed off to college. In many ways he was reminding me not to get too arrogant because I was going off to a predominately white school. Deep down inside, I now know he was warning me not to think for a second that I could do what white kids were doing. I was still Black in America. He was protecting me and my heart.

It was also here that I believe I started formulated my views about equity. I was seeing the inside of a world that most Black kids weren't seeing. I was learning about corporate politics, networking and even the power of informal leadership right on my college campus. I knew quickly that not knowing how all of this worked was a disadvantage to many kids of color. I learned how this could ultimately impact the economics of entire communities. Not being "in the know "was dangerous. I wanted everyone to know how the system *really* worked so everyone would have the opportunity to be successful.

Your Musings:

_____

_____

_____

_____

_____

_____

_____

_____

_____

_____

_____

_____

_____

_____

_____

_____

_____

_____

_____

_____

_____

_____

> "If we can't talk about race, we simply create version 2.0 of what we already have. I'm not interested in that model. "

The Night the World Changed

Ishould have known that this day would change my life. I felt it from the minute I woke up with one of my infamous function-like-it-doesn't-hurt migraines. It was a beautiful February day; brisk and beautiful as most Atlanta winter days are. I had plenty to do this day; menial tasks, but nevertheless, plenty to do. Things like grocery shopping, getting my hair done and maybe even squeezing in a manicure, were the order of the day. The day, in all its beauty, didn't match how much physical pain I was in, but when I was growing up, my father always encouraged me to let my migraines know who was boss. So, I proceeded with my day. I was the boss.

My father had settled into retirement in some odd ways. He had decided to run a few booths at a local flea market. His chief joy was collecting treasures (in my mom's words, AKA for junk!) from estate sales and garage sales and selling them in his booth at the flea market. To my mother's dismay, some of these treasures made their way to our house stored and organized in our two-car garage… ultimately, making room for only one car.

As I was running errands, I stopped by the flea market to do my ceremonial "drop in and say hello" to my father and all of his friends at the flea market. My father was there; all smiles as usual. My father always acted like he had not seen me in years. I loved this. I visited with my father for about 30 minutes and then told him I had to go. As I was leaving he said, "I'll see you later on." I told my father

143

he would not see me later, as I was going to stay in for the evening once I got home. He repeated, "I'll see you later." He was right. I did see him later.

About 9 pm that same night, my phone rang at home. I answered it and heard nothing but unintelligible screams from my mother. I could make out "your dad, your dad." That is all I could understand. The rest was a blur. I just remember jumping in my car and making the short 7-minute drive to their house. When I arrived, I was blinded by the flashing lights of both a fire truck and ambulance at our house. I ran in the house and up the stairs only to be held back by a paramedic. The door to my parent's bedroom was closed. The paramedic said my dad was in good hands; they were working on him. They believed he may have had another heart attack. Neighbors seemed to flocking in. Everywhere I looked there was yet another concerned neighbor standing somewhere in the house. Everyone loved my father.

The paramedics moved my father to the ambulance. I had a sinking feeling that my father was dead. I knew because I felt like someone had sucked the oxygen right out of the atmosphere. I could feel and breathe the difference. His presence in the world changed the world. I felt like the world had actually stopped moving and functioning. I jumped in my car and raced to the hospital. I joined my mother and grandmother there. My grandmother didn't drive and had somehow gotten on a bus at night to get to the hospital to be with us. We were sitting in the chapel. Waiting. Waiting for someone to tell us something. My mother was hysterical and looked at me with a sorrow I cannot describe. She said, "I think your daddy is dead." I was stoic and remained optimistic. Until the doctor came in to tell us…my father was dead.

When I look back, I realize my father died when he was the age I am right now. He died too young. My life changed forever that day. My grandmother knew my that life changed forever that day, too. There was a lot of chaos at the hospital. People were now rushing there to be at my mother's side. Though I was now in my early 20's, I felt like an infant in that moment. No capacity to help anyone. Constance Elizabeth Hancock, my grandmother, was one of the most important people in my life. My grandmother tapped me on the shoulder and said, "You and me, we're going to go back home. We're leaving all of them at the hospital and we're going back home." In my own hysteria I said, "Grandma, why do we have to go back home right now?" She said, "Just trust me."

This was the middle of the night. So, we went back to my parent's house. We went back to their bedroom. The room where my father had just died. My grandmother asked me to get on the other side of the bed to help her flip the mattress over. I said, "Grandma really? Now? You need to flip the mattress over? She said, "Yes, just flip it over." So, there we were flipping this gigantic king-sized mattress over to the other side. Together, two distinctly different generations of Black women were there flipping a mattress. We flipped it over and changed the linens and made up the bed. It was almost like nothing happened there.

When my mother returned from the hospital, she was still in shock. I whispered over to my grandmother, "Why did we need to flip the mattress over?" She said, "That's where the stain was. I didn't want your mother to be a part of the stain of what she had just gone through so we flipped it over." I have kept that memory right here in the frontal lobes all of my life. How often is the "stain" of our pain right on the other side of where we stand, sit or lie? Just flipped over so we don't have to see it.

Living in Atlanta, I was fortunate to have grown up in the company of great civil rights leaders. Growing up, my pastor was the civil rights icon, Rev. Dr. Ralph David Abernathy. He had a very large presence, but I don't think as young people, we had any idea how big he really was. Sure, we knew he marched with Dr. Martin

Luther King, Jr. We even saw the King family at our church. But, I just don't think we knew how iconic Rev. Abernathy was. That is, until my father died.

Unlike me, my mother and grandparents, my father was not a church-goer. He didn't have anything against religion. He just didn't trust preachers. He said those tithes and offerings were what they used to buy their new Cadillacs. My mother would come unglued every time my father would say something like that. She said it was a terrible bias that my father had, but he had no trouble letting us know about it.

When my father died, my mother insisted that he have a church funeral. I found that odd since my father rarely set foot in a church. My mother said it was tradition; that West Hunter Street Baptist Church had been in our family for several generations. You got married there and you were funeralized there. Decision made. The funeral was being planned and the whole time I knew, even in death, my father was being put in a position he would not have chosen. He wouldn't have had a traditional funeral. He wouldn't have been in a church. He would have had jazz and blues music playing. He would have been buried in his favorite blue mechanics jumpsuit – the one he always wore even though he knew nothing about fixing a car. Instead, he was a part of following tradition; the thing he taught me to challenge.

The funeral was formal, serene and elegant - not reflective of my father's personality or style. However, in grief you sort of forget about all of that. Your heart aches so bad you can't remember anything but the pain. The suit he was wearing, the formality of the service and even the absence of many of his poker buddies was in stark contrast to the man I knew. I realized that even death can force you to be something that you're not. I began to wonder at what point we would be able to be free.

After we left the cemetery, I felt like my heart had been

ripped out and replaced with darkness. My beacon of light had been snuffed out and I felt as if I were no longer anchored in the world. Every childhood story and experience seemed intricately linked to my father and he was gone. I questioned my entire identity and wondered if the chapters of my life had somehow died along with him.

When I got back to my parent's house, everywhere I looked were people. Every room and every corner had someone in it. It was all a reflection of the love people had for my father, but it was too much to bear. I made my way solemnly through the crowd and headed upstairs to my parent's room; the room where my father died. I laid across the bed and for the first time since my father died, I sobbed uncontrollably. All of the pain that I had held inside in order to be strong for my mother was coming out. I could not control it. I felt like I was dying, too. The longer I cried, the more I felt like my history was being erased. My father ignited my curiosity, my creativity and my wonder. How could I be me without him? The tears wouldn't stop and I felt like I couldn't breathe. As I lay sobbing, head buried in the bed, I felt someone lay down beside me. I didn't have the strength to see who it was. I was too devastated to care. I assumed it was someone from the sea of people downstairs just coming in to check on me. I didn't want to be checked on. I wanted to be left alone. I didn't acknowledge the presence of the person who had joined me on the bed. I didn't even lift my head to see who it was. I continued to sob.

Then, I heard a familiar voice. A very familiar voice. It was the voice of Rev. Dr. Ralph David Abernathy. His voice was strong and regal and his words were even more profound than his voice. He said, "Why are you crying?" I couldn't believe it. Why was I crying? What kind of question was that? I didn't answer. It seemed such a silly question to ask. Before I could make sense of his question, he added "There is no reason to cry. Didn't you have a great father?" I answered softly, "yes." Then he said, "did he do great things in the world?" Again, I answered softly, "yes." Lastly, he said, "didn't he teach you some amazing things?" I rolled over in the bed and looked at Rev. Abernathy and said, "Yes. He taught me almost everything I know."

At that point, Rev. Abernathy got up from the bed and stood in front of me. He then said, "Well, stop crying. Your father has equipped you to carry on some great things. Now get to work." He then left the room. Leaving me to think about my tears in an entirely different way.

Rev. Dr. Ralph D. Abernathy, the civil rights giant who marched side-by-side with Dr. Martin Luther King, Jr. just told me to, "Get to work."

And so, I did.

AFTERWORD

A lot of people are talking about the words diversity, inclusion, equity, equality, fairness and justice. We want all of these things in the world and the confusion around "how" to do it has created a word confusion that keeps us from fully understanding the delineation between the words. It is critical that we begin to tease out the definitions of the words so we understand our own actions, what they reflect
in our behaviors and systems and ultimately, how to accomplish necessary factors in each of the words.

White People Really Love Salad is a journey into how our thinking is shaped at a very young age. Among many things, it explores the power of parents, informal "villages," access opportunities, the gravity of words and relationships and ultimately, the power that children can have in influencing all of it. Each story provides us with an important opportunity to pause and reflect on why we think an behave in the ways we do.

I believe equity, inclusion and diversity work is work that operates like gears and exists on a continuum. We never really get finished with any of it. Each body of work is contingent upon the next. If you stop doing diversity work, inclusiveness fails. If you don't focus on equality, equity cannot be realized. They are each different, but rely on the other for survival.

At the foundation of all of this is our own thinking. Our own lenses for seeing the world. My goal in writing the book was to get you thinking, as I did, about the earliest sources of your thinking and actions. That has everything to do with what you will do next. I wish you the best on that journey.

It's Your Move.